PRAISE FOR

HOODOO CLEANSING AND PROTECTION MAGIC

"If you think all books on cleansin[...] as watching paint dry, think aga[...] what I'd never thought possible: a book on the subject that's not only relatable and fun to read but also filled with expert advice from a practitioner who truly knows her stuff. Destined to become a classic, *Hoodoo Cleansing and Protection Magic* should be a part of every magical class curriculum and have a spot near every working altar. It's a valuable tool that no practitioner can afford to be without!"

> —DOROTHY MORRISON, author of *Utterly Wicked*

"*Hoodoo Cleansing and Protection Magic* by Miss Aida is a masterful blend of personal anecdotes and work accompanied by the perfect psalm for every occasion. In twenty years of practicing Hoodoo, I found this to be one of the best books I've read. Give this book a prominent place on the shelf; you'll be needing it."

> —AMY BLACKTHORN, owner of Blackthorn Hoodoo Blends and author of *Blackthorn's Botanical Magic* and *Sacred Smoke*

"By showing us numerous ways of using Hoodoo to cleanse negative energies and entities, Miss Aida helps us live a life of clarity and quality. Her personal stories and straightforward writing pull you in and let you know exactly what to do. Miss Aida has created a very useful addition to the literature that involves Hoodoo."

> —STEPHANIE ROSE BIRD, author of numerous books including the award-winning *Sticks, Stones, Roots, and Bones* and *Out of the Blue*

"Miss Aida's *Hoodoo Cleansing and Protection Magic* is a book that many other authors would like to have written, however few possess the knowledge and experience, as well as the patience, to have done so. The formulas shared in *Hoodoo Cleansing and Protection Magic* are as complete and extensive as they are incredible. My favorite parts of this book are the explanations of the form, use, and tradition for each one. The clarity of Miss Aida's vision allows her to express herself in a way that makes this book easy to understand for readers of any experience level."

—ELHOIM LEOFAR, author of *The Magical
Art of Crafting Charm Bags*

"Miss Aida offers a plethora of Hoodoo protective practices: everything you need to know to protect yourself contained in one book! If you are just getting started, make this book your pocket bible. Keep it with your paranormal gear, tarot cards, reiki table, vending items. . . . I wish she had written *Hoodoo Cleansing and Protection Magic* when I started my journey. I'm totally wearing my dime anklet right now!"

—KRISTIN LEE, proprietress of the Bellaire
House, author of *1699 Belmont Street*, and
paranormal investigator

"In *Hoodoo Cleansing and Protection Magic*, her comprehensive guidebook, Miss Aida offers newcomers, practitioners, and adepts alike secrets that were passed down to her through her family. Her rituals are refreshingly practical, and she interweaves them with entertaining and enlightening personal anecdotes. By the end of this book, the reader will have learned to banish negative energies through rootwork, washes, and the art of Hoodoo. An authoritative work on this difficult and taboo topic was long overdue, and Miss Aida's candor and spice greatly add to its appeal."

—LAWREN LEO, author of *Horse Magick*

"*Hoodoo Cleansing and Protection Magic* is the book I've wanted for decades and never found—until now. Miss Aida provides insight into how dark forces manifest within us and in our world, but also teaches us how to work positively toward removing negative energy. Tapping into the divine power she finds in nature, fire, water, oils, herbs, crystals and stones, she demonstrates the powerful magic that manifests when elements come together. By combining rituals and practices of diverse religious traditions with decades of experience in working with all forms of negative energy, Miss Aida provides everything needed to remove powers of negativity affecting us. For practitioners and seekers alike, Miss Aida's *Hoodoo Cleansing and Protection Magic* is an invaluable guide and a comfort."

—KAROL JACKOWSKI, author of *Sister Karol's Book of Spells, Blessings, and Folk Magic* and other books

"Miss Aida is a gifted Conjure worker and writer. People often forget about the importance of cleansing and protecting themselves, their homes, and possessions when it comes to their Hoodoo/Conjure practice. In her book, *Hoodoo Cleansing and Protection Magic*, Miss Aida reminds us why these steps are necessary. I loved this book and will be using it as a reference in my Hoodoo classes."

—YVETTE WYATT, the Motown Witch

"*Hoodoo Cleansing and Protection Magic* has all the right ingredients for the practical and the mystical. It helps make sense of when your intuition tells you that you need protection and what to do about it. Essential as a reference and DIY guide for the well-versed, as well as those new to Hoodoo."

—MARLENE PARDO PELLICER, author of *Supernatural Safety*

"In these pages, Miss Aida shares foundational truths that—regardless of your own spiritual practice—will help you. Follow her advice and clearly outlined workings to avoid many of the pitfalls experienced by new and even experienced spiritual workers. Miss Aida's book will stand the test of time for those seeking to understand the importance of developing a consistent spiritual hygiene practice. *Hoodoo Cleansing and Protection Magic* is now part of my personal working library and sure to be a reference guide for years to come."

—ANDREA WESTON, owner and operator of *Ambrozine Legare Conjure*, Root-worker, Diviner, and Palera

"*Hoodoo Cleansing and Protection Magic* is an absolute must for beginners and adepts alike, covering foundational knowledge that's too often unknown, skipped, or overlooked. Miss Aida provides a number of easy-to-use-and-understand recipes and cleanses to get readers started. Written in a way that gives thorough understanding and information about negative energy and its many sources—including places, things, and people—crucially, Miss Aida also gives important advice as to when self-help is not enough, and professionals must be called in. Additionally, she provides essential information for those who are ill and their caregivers—people who are exposed to negative energy on a regular and constant basis. Her book is filled with real stories and a warm tone. Definitely a foundational manual for new Spiritualists."

—PAPA HECTOR SALVA, author of
The 21 Divisions

"I was immediately drawn in by Miss Aida's self-awareness and dry sense of humor. I nodded and laughed out loud at the accounts of her personal experiences, because they are so relatable. The clinician in me appreciates her preventative approach and clear instructions on how to assess and monitor for negative energy, entities, and people. The folk magician in me appreciates the many methods she shares to effectively get rid of them. Miss Aida generously shares with her readers her family's customs as well as a lifetime of her own personal experiences. *Hoodoo Cleansing and Protection Magic* contains both practical and easy-to-execute fundamentals of spiritual hygiene that everyone should be practicing."

—MARY-GRACE FAHRUN, author of *Italian
Folk Magic*

HOODOO CLEANSING

AND PROTECTION MAGIC

Banish Negative Energy
AND
Ward Off Unpleasant People

MISS AIDA

Foreword by Judika Illes

WEISER BOOKS

This edition first published in 2020 by Weiser Books, an imprint of
Red Wheel/Weiser, LLC
With offices at:
65 Parker Street, Suite 7
Newburyport, MA 01950
www.redwheelweiser.com

ISBN: 978-1-57863-697-6
Library of Congress Cataloging-in-Publication Data available upon
request.

Cover design by Kathryn Sky-Peck
Interior by Happenstance Type-O-Rama
Typeset in Walbaum, Dress, and Rumble

Printed in the United States of America
IBI

10 9 8 7 6 5 4 3 2 1

This book is dedicated in loving
memory to my parents,
Nick Catel and Kiriaki Catel.

CONTENTS

FOREWORD

I did not set out to be a metaphysical author, even though I have been studying and practicing the magical arts for most of my life. My pursuits were originally intended for myself alone, solely for my own use, joy, and pleasure. Eventually, however, a publisher asked me whether I would like to write a book on spellcasting. It was an opportunity and I seized it. After I agreed, the publisher informed me that my book would be titled *Earth Mother Magic*, gave me a deadline for submission, and told me to go write.

Although I was very happy, that title sparked a personal dilemma. On one hand, writing a guide to spellcasting was not difficult for me; the topic is one in which I am well-versed. On the other hand, there were already so many spellbooks. The market was awash with them. Did anyone need another? Especially one whose title implied an ecological orientation? How could I justify cutting down trees to make paper for just another book reiterating the same old material already found in so many other books? After some deliberation, I determined that the only way was to write the most truthful and accurate book that I could, one that didn't replicate other information easily found elsewhere.

Long before I was a writer of books about magic, I was a devoted reader of such books. Because I am not merely a reader, but also a practitioner, I am able to recognize that some are by authors who have likely never actually cast the spells they write about in their books. They're bluffing. These books are full of evocative but incomplete instructions or—even worse—instructions that could not actually be put into practice. Imagine a cookbook whose recipes produced inedible results rather than delicious dishes. An inexperienced reader might think their inability to follow directions was their own fault, when, in fact, it is the author's.

However, in the same way that I can recognize a metaphysical author who does not really know their stuff, I can also recognize a master of the craft. Miss Aida is the real deal. *Hoodoo Cleansing and Protection Magic* is the work of an expert, someone who brings years of experience and learning to her book and is also able to write with clarity and humor, so that her words are invaluable to others. This book is a treasure that will benefit experienced practitioner and neophyte alike, a valuable asset for all practitioners and would-be practitioners.

It is not often that an author causes me to gasp aloud with sudden revelation, but Miss Aida has done so. (I will never look at welcome mats the same way again. Read this book and learn.) Those who learn exclusively from books, or who have only had one teacher, often have limited magical vision. Miss Aida demonstrates how to create a potent body of knowledge based on the totality of your life's experiences. Deriving from a family whose members practiced Santeria, Palo, and *brujeria*, as well as combinations of these traditions, she draws upon these practices, as well as her own professional expertise, both magical and mundane, to create a body of work that will benefit *anyone* seeking assistance with spiritual cleansing and protection.

As any metaphysical practitioner worth their salt will tell you, cleansing and protection work should be general practice for *everyone*, although more so for some, something that Miss Aida explains in this book. They are crucial components of everyone's magical practice. Regardless of what types of spells you seek to cast; regardless how happy or challenging your life might be, cleansing and protection will enhance your ability to achieve your life's goals.

The magical world does not exist apart from the mundane. They work best and most powerfully together, hand in hand. (Classic example: you can cast all the employment spells in the world but if you are not simultaneously seeking work—or at least checking your phone or email, so that you can respond to offers—they won't work.) *Hoodoo Cleansing and Protection Magic* incorporates knowledge Miss Aida has amassed in her extensive career as a medical professional. I don't know of any other magical book that does this or at least so effectively. Within these pages, you will find information for self-cleansing, as well as for cleansing your home and other spaces. Miss Aida advises you how to forestall danger, offering tips for how to alert yourself to the presence of negative and toxic people, and how to protect yourself from them. She offers special instructions for those whose need for cleansing and protection may be greater than the norm, such as spiritual workers, caregivers, and those requiring care. She provides a thirteen-day eradication ritual that will benefit all and also teaches you how to recognize when your situation may require professional help.

Miss Aida's *Hoodoo Cleansing and Protection Magic* is not just another book reiterating the same old, same old material easily found elsewhere, but one that is unique, powerful, and timeless. I am so pleased to welcome you to what is sure to become a classic.

—JUDIKA ILLES, author of
Encyclopedia of 5,000 Spells

ACKNOWLEDGMENTS

First and foremost, my heartfelt gratitude is extended to Judika Illes, who has the soul of an angel and the patience of a saint. Judika has mentored me from the time when this book proposal was merely an idea, throughout the project, and up to the very end. She has become a good friend and someone that I truly adore and respect.

Russell Azbill, an award-winning author as well as a MUFON field investigator and paranormal investigator, has been my virtual life support throughout this book project. Investigator Azbill had helped me tremendously in all areas relating to paranormal activities, in addition to assisting me with proper authorship. He had also graciously shared some of his knowledge with all of us in an exclusive interview, found later in this book.

Rabbi Geoffrey Dennis, the author of *The Encyclopedia of Jewish Myth, Magic, and Mysticism,* has also graciously granted an interview in order to familiarize us with the Jewish belief systems as they relate to human possession. Rabbi Dennis is a phenomenal teacher as well as an all-around great guy. If it weren't for the perseverance of Steven Rossmoore, MD, who has been a dear friend for over a decade, I never would have known to contact the Rabbi for this valuable information.

Thank you to Gordon Ireland, who patiently helped me with my persistent questions regarding Paganism; Mary-Beth K. (aka Motha MaryBeth), for her friendship, encouragement, and proofreading; and Lucy Chu, my spiritual daughter, who made herself available for any help needed with proper grammar and construction.

My fur-babies, Asha-Maria, Junior, and Wolfie, patiently forfeited a good amount of playtime in order for their Mommy to write this book. Thank you for your sacrifice!

Most importantly, thank you to my loving clients for your enduring loyalty and support.

INTRODUCTION

Everything in this world has a balance of both positive and negative influences. But often when we encounter negative energies, negative behaviors in others, or negative forces, it leads to a downward spiral of one negative event following another.

Take, for example, the proverbial "run of bad luck" that most of us have encountered. It begins with something not going the way we expected. Following the initial unpleasant results, a trickle-down effect has everything else going wrong as well. Unless we have a normally happy life to return to with people or events that bring pleasure to break out of all the negativity hanging around, we will continue on a downward slope in which absolutely nothing goes as planned. We can get immersed in negativity, which, in turn, attracts more of the same.

What about arguments? Often when we argue with one person, it will then seem as if everybody wants to take a jab at us too. We may find ourselves thinking, "What is wrong with everybody?" The reality is that there's something wrong with us because we are the ones who have gotten immersed in an invisible flood of aggressive negativity. With all these unfavorable vibrations collecting around us, others will see us as the source of the threat and their instinctive response may be to fight as a form of protection. The end result is that even more aggressive negativity soon surrounds us.

Negative forces can affect us in many ways ranging from mild potencies, such as feeling drained or having a run of bad luck, to severe spiritual attacks. Throughout my life, friends, clients, and even strangers have approached me to ask for help when something just didn't feel right or normal. Sometimes they had general concerns regarding feeling run-down or spiritual discomfort. At other times they were concerned with sensations of a "strangeness" in their self-perception or spiritual well-being. There may have been an unexplainable spate of back luck or endless obstacles were cropping up in their paths causing nothing to work out for them.

Unfortunately, in the severer cases many relayed that their friends or associates suddenly treated them poorly, leaving them to suffer the stigma of an outcast. There might be inexplicable feelings of impending doom. In some instances, many suspected that they had been cursed by somebody. In the worst-case scenarios, they have had unwanted visits by unseen negative forces.

Illness, whether physical or emotional, is a noteworthy example of how negativity can and will draw in more of the same unfavorable energies and worsen an initial condition. More often than not, not understanding an existing disease and how to alleviate some of the uncomfortable symptoms produces feelings of helplessness, hopelessness, and fears of the unknown. These dynamics, in turn, produce isolation, bitterness, and/or anger.

What happens next? The consequences produce a vicious cycle of emotional distress, thus generating further physiological injuries. When the body and mind veer away from normalcy, it damages spiritual well-being. These victims are now attracting and being surrounded by more negative forces, while their significant others and/or caregivers become vulnerable and susceptible to the same because they are in the line of fire.

Negative and positive forces are equally balanced in our world. Sadly, this concept also applies to people. Good people assume that everyone possesses good qualities, and despite exhibited inappropriate behaviors, many of us desperately struggle to see the good in everybody. Conversely, the bad ones see good people as pawns or patsies and interpret their values and demeanors as a sign of weakness. These bad people are often predators, such as narcissists, sociopaths, thieves, liars, con artists, scammers, abusers, etc., who are looking for prey in hopes of stealing something of value:

* The narcissists and sociopaths may wish to steal social or work status, a significant other, or family.

* The abusers wish to take away the freedom, self-worth, and/or self-esteem of others.

* Con artists, scammers, and thieves will strive to obtain material possessions and/or sexual gratification. These people are usually thrill seekers who lack a conscience and use people to achieve their self-serving goals.

Once such predators target their victims, they immediately, and masterfully, begin to manipulate and minimize their victims' sense of control. Little by little, they empower themselves by robbing their targets of their self-esteem, leaving the victims doubting themselves and fearful and thus forcing them to rely on the predator for a never-to-be-realized redemption or recovery. Instead, during the entire process, the victims' sense of well-being is compromised both emotionally and spiritually, making them vulnerable to further harm wherever negative forces are present.

Unwanted spiritual visitations are one of the most terrifying experiences you may have. They also produce the worst of the physiological-emotional-spiritual imbalances due to the instinctive fight-or-flight mechanism that kicks in when we are threatened. While this response tells the adrenal glands to produce extra adrenaline in order to act quickly, most people will not know how to fight off an entity and many others are unable to run away. As a result of this inability to react effectively, the adrenal glands continue to pump out adrenaline, which is a severe physiological stressor, and this negatively affects a person's interrelated health, emotional, and spiritual balance.

These are just a few examples of the most common types of negative situations that we may encounter. However, other scenarios will be discussed as they come up later in this book. Just remember that no matter what the situation might be—whether there is opposition toward our well-being delivered by people or their energies all the way to emotionally harmful spiritual encounters—it can happen to the best of us!

Without an idea of why these events are occurring and how to combat them, we lose control. If we don't move past this vulnerability, we will invite, support, and nurture subsequent occurrences. When we are continuously and helplessly stricken with undesirable stimuli, it is debilitating and thus promotes weakness and susceptibility to further harm.

However, there are always means to counterattack! Everyone and everything has their own vulnerabilities, and we will explore those weaknesses and learn to prevail over negative influences with spellwork, prayer, and adjusting our own behaviors. Additionally, we will explore ways to deter or prevent future occurrences. By examining the causes that brought forth the negative people, events, or forces, we find enough knowledge to avoid future encounters.

We will explore not only my personal experiences in conquering negative forces, but also those of my many beloved clients who have graciously consented to share their stories. I would like to begin with one of my own short stories now.

Introduction

In my younger days, I thought that God must have made me a human magnet for strangers with problems. They would stop me in parking lots, in stores, at the beauty shop—you name it—to tell me all about their difficulties. These events were not only unwelcome, but also emotionally taxing. And yet, something prompted me to listen to them and offer sound spiritual and psychological advice.

One day when I returned home from an exhausting encounter with a stranger, I asked my mother, a witch: "Why do people always come to me, out of the clear blue sky, and pour out their problems in search of answers?" She explained to me first in Spanish that God had gifted us all with a brilliant light that surrounds each and every one of us. We can subconsciously—and sometimes consciously— see that light around others. When people are in a bad way, that light becomes dim because it's weighed down or even damaged with bad energies. When they see that others have brilliant ones, they are subconsciously attracted to them in hopes of replenishing their own.

Then, in her broken English she concluded by saying: "But, you be careful because the bad ones who know about the light will try to throw their garbage on yours. Now, you go spray you-self with Agua Florida (Florida Water) before all these problems that this stranger have stick to you."

What was this sweet little ole Cuban witch talking about? She was talking about the aura and insuring that it is cared for. . . .

1

It Begins with the Aura

Have you ever seen paintings of God or saints or revered deities with a glow surrounding their heads? These depictions of light are energy fields called *auras*, something all matter and living beings possess. The radiance of the aura can emit different degrees of brightness or dim luminosity, as well as emanating different colors.

Auras act as shields, protecting us from outside negative influences that might affect our psychological and spiritual well-being. In many cultures and traditions, it is also believed that the aura protects our physiological status. There are thousands of depictions, especially in Eastern cultures, of radiance emitting from the chakras.

In the book *How to See and Read the Aura*, author Ted Andrews explains that the healthier we are, both emotionally and physically, the more vitalized our auras become, and, therefore, they will emit a stronger radiance. In other words, a healthy and happy lifestyle nourishes our auras. Unfortunately, when we are in a state of emotional or physiological "dis-ease," our auras do not receive needed sustenance and become weakened and subdued.

Sometimes we can consciously see auras. This is especially true for children and those of us who are empaths or have been trained to do so. However, all of us unconsciously sense them. Numerous psychologists have told me that an abusive man can walk into a room with more than one hundred women and choose his next victim without any conversation. Although scientists call this an "unexplained phenomenon," those of us in spiritual practices know that such an abuser can simply sense a suppressed or darkened aura. This explains why domestic violence victims will usually enter one abusive relationship after another if they lack the resources for professional help. It's usually because they were "chosen" time and again by savvy victimizers.

We have a symbiotic relationship with our auras. If we take care of our aura, our aura will take care of us! A healthy and radiant aura will easily ward off minute undesirable forces and sustain our existing conditions, but we must, in turn, keep our auras healthy to maintain the protection that they provide. Therefore, it is imperative to be familiar with stimuli that may attack or even injure our precious shield.

Everyday Nuisances that Affect Your Shield

Simple attacks on the aura consist of any stimuli that disrupt our feelings of security, comfort, well-being, and normalcy. Such events leave us feeling invaded but not harmed. Think of it in terms of just having washed and waxed your car. Feeling proud of its clean and shiny appearance, you take it out for a drive but run it through mud. Your level of comfort has been upset because the car is dirty again—what a nuisance!—but it's unharmed.

Common events or everyday negativity that upset us along these lines may include, but are not limited to:

* **Arguments and insults:** There are so many types of insults possible in our societies and they vary from verbal cues to nonverbal gestures. Everyday arguments at home, on the road, at work, etc., are attacks on the aura.

* **Envy:** Envy is a negative emotion experienced by people who believe that they deserve what someone else has. Unfortunately, people who give in to this emotion might treat their targets with rudeness, arrogance, cruelty, and intrigue. They may even gossip about and slander those they envy. Yes, we know who they are because we can always sense their negativity—and that very negativity is also an attack on our aura.

* **Jealousy:** This emotion must involve more than one person because it's a threat, either real or perceived, to another person's relationship. In other words, a person will view you as the threat to their existing or desired relationship. Jealousy will also trigger similar behaviors as that of envy and cause the same results to our shields.

* **Entitlement:** Unfortunately, we can encounter people who are just plain mean, rude, and nasty; they have superiority complexes. They also lack respect and consideration for others, their boundaries, their hardships, and their need for self-preservation. Their presence causes extreme discomfort because they disrupt our sense of well-being.

* **Prejudice and scapegoating:** Ignorance obviously causes prejudice, and this will lead to blaming the

victim for the wrongdoing of others. Blame comes in many forms, from secretive or clandestine expressions in which the target becomes an outcast to open verbal or physical attacks. Even when nothing is said, the aura can sense the blame being casted. The "evil eye," a gaze or stare accompanied by malicious thoughts, is one form of transmitting nonverbal spiritual attacks.

* **Mercury in Retrograde:** Mercury is the planet that fosters communication. Three or four times a year, for a three-week period, it will appear to be moving in the opposite direction viewed from Earth. During retrograde, there is interference with direct or technological channels of communication. We will find that people either don't understand the verbal messages that we are conveying or we misunderstand them. Often, computers break down or there is trouble with telephone transmissions. Whatever the interruptions are, we are left in a state of frustration and irritability.

* **Psychic vampires:** These are the people who will pour out their problems into any compassionate soul lending them an ear. Whether intentionally or unintentionally, by the time that they have completely purged, they will walk away feeling refreshed and renewed, because they have stolen our vitalities, while leaving us feeling completely drained. It is as though they have sucked the life force right out of us. They have consumed the energy from our auras, thus, the term "psychic vampires."

Haven't we all fallen victim to at least a few of these incidents? The episodes usually leave us surprised, taken aback, angered, fearful, or in other states veering from normalcy. Our auras are slightly injured, and this will show up in our behaviors, our body language, and both the aura's color and degree of radiance.

When our auras are attacked, we are subconsciously aware of the fact that something is wrong. However, if we are not consciously focusing on the fact that it is indeed our shield that has been affected, the injury instead manifests as a questioning of our own feelings of security, self-esteem, and self-worth. These doubts, in turn, will make us vulnerable to further attacks from those who may intend us harm.

Additionally, we can also hurt ourselves by inviting further injuries. The adage "Anything that could possibly go wrong will go wrong," called Murphy's Law, kicks in for spiritual injuries. What is happening is that we ourselves are inviting that bad luck. If we have had two or more consecutive attacks, we may believe that we are having a run of bad luck. If we truly believe it, then it is an inappropriate affirmation and it becomes an invitation for additional unfortunate incidents to occur.

Immediate cleansing of the aura after disruptive stimuli is imperative. Subsequent protection of the aura is of equal importance. It is as easy as taking a bath. What happens when we are dirty and in desperate need of a bath? Our motivation and self-esteem are slightly diminished. Our behaviors are sluggish, and our body language expresses our discomfort with poor posture. This, in turn, makes us vulnerable to the belief that our existing condition is offensive to others, and because that is our affirmation, others will treat us accordingly. After bathing, we feel refreshed, rejuvenated, and our self-esteem improves. Our body language changes to express the self-confidence we feel. Bathing eradicates the damage imposed from being dirty and prevents further harm.

Cleansing and protecting the aura will repair the injury brought on by minor attacks. A refreshed and protected aura, in turn, will provide us with the optimal spiritual immunity possible. It is our spiritual bath!

Cleaning the Aura of Minor Attacks

With so many diverse spiritual and religious practices from around the world, it would be virtually impossible to list every imaginable technique of aura cleansing in this chapter. Therefore, with the utmost respect to all the practitioners of every faith, the listed techniques are those that I have personally found to be successful for minor attacks.

Please keep in mind that whether your intention is called an affirmation, petition, command, or something else, it is important to state it aloud with both conviction and confidence. Doing so not only tells your own brain, body, Spirit Guides, and Guardian Angels what must be done, but it also aids in surrounding yourself with helpful vibrations and energies.

Florida Water

Considered a cologne by the manufacturers, Florida Water was originally introduced in the United States in the 1800s. It was named after the Fountain of Youth allegedly located in the state of Florida. This amazing cologne is also available in other continents including South America, Central America, and Asia. It has an appealing fragrance that can be worn by both men and women.

Practitioners of Hoodoo, Wicca, Santería, Voodoo, and other faiths often utilize Florida Water in ritual offerings, purification ceremonies, and the cleansing of negative energies for a person, object, or area. Some practitioners even use it in lieu of Holy Water for Blessing Rites.

Simply pour the Florida Water into a previously unused spray bottle. Starting from the crown of your head and working downward to your feet, spray yourself from top to bottom—which is a symbolic gesture of making something go away—while stating aloud, with each spray, that negativity will leave you and your aura is cleansed.

You may also spray your surrounding area if negative energies have attached themselves to something in your dwelling. However, be mindful that Florida Water has an alcohol base. Be careful not to spray wood, leather, or other materials that can be damaged by alcohol.

Usually, a feeling of rejuvenation will occur immediately. If not, repeat the process.

Holy Water

This is water that has been blessed by a religious or spiritual leader, consecrated by a revered spiritual deity, or comes from the first rain in the month of May. Mainly used as a spiritual cleansing agent, it is also utilized in both Blessing and Protection Rites.

If you don't have access to a religious or spiritual leader or May's rainwater, the easiest way to acquire Holy Water is to visit a Roman Catholic, Anglican, or Eastern Christian (such as Orthodox) church and request it. Bring a clean, empty bottle, preferably one that previously contained purified water, such as a brand-name purified, distilled, or filtered water and ask for it to be filled with Holy Water. (Do not use bottles that used to contain mineral water.)

My preferred Holy Water is from Lourdes, France, where the Virgin Mary has a consecrated grotto. It is a little costly, but this water, in my opinion, has performed near-miracles.

Please do not buy Holy Water from questionable sources. There was once a botanica that sold their dirty, used altar water as Holy Water. It had an offensive odor and was visibly mucky. Some companies will just bottle water and call it Holy Water. Since it is impossible to know if the water is legitimate, it is safer to obtain it from the types of reputable sources I've mentioned here.

Once you have your Holy Water, keep it refrigerated. There is a bacterium called *Pseudomonas aeruginosa* naturally found in many types of drinking water. Since bacteria multiply in warm, dark environments, we want to keep the water refrigerated, as we do with any other perishables to keep the bacteria count at a safe level.

Just as with the Florida Water, simply pour the Holy Water into a previously unused and clean spray bottle. Starting from the crown of your head and working downward to your feet, spray yourself from top to bottom—a symbolic gesture of making something go away—while stating aloud with each spray that negativity will leave you and your aura is cleansed and protected.

Unlike Florida Water, Holy Water will not damage wood, leather, or other materials. Therefore, it is safe to lightly spray it in your dwelling or places where negativity may have attached itself. Do this while demanding that all negativity leave the area at once.

Repeating the process at any time is never harmful. It can only help.

Rue Water

Rue (*Ruta graveolens*), also called the herb of grace, is an herb that has been used since ancient times to protect against and ward off witchcraft.

In the early Catholic churches, rue was employed alongside Holy Water to wash away sins. It was subsequently recognized by varied spiritual faiths for other magical properties, including its ability to rid a person or space of negative energies.

Practitioners of many spiritual faiths including Wicca, Hoodoo, Santería, and Palo, to name but a few, all acknowledge the importance of rue. In the book *Brazilian Palo Primer,* Robert Laremy talked about how it wards off the evil eye and has protective properties. He states: "All practitioners of Kimbanda keep plenty of rue around." Personally, I always keep at least five pounds of it in my own household!

However, if you are a nursing mother, pregnant, or actively trying to conceive, *do not* work with this herb. Rue is abortifacient, causing uterine contractions, and could ultimately lead to a miscarriage.

As with all herbs, first bless the rue. This is easy. Just place a tablespoon in your hand. Then recite a blessing prayer or just state that by your own power, you bless this herb. A common Hoodoo practice is to recite Psalm 23 aloud over most herbs:

PSALM 23

1 The LORD is my shepherd; I shall not want.

2 He maketh me to lie down in green pastures: he leadeth me beside the still waters.

3 He restoreth my soul: he leadeth me in the paths of righteousness for his name's sake.

4 Yea, though I walk through the valley of the shadow of death, I will fear no evil: for thou art with me; thy rod and thy staff they comfort me.

5 Thou preparest a table before me in the presence of mine enemies: thou anointest my head with oil; my cup runneth over.

6 Surely goodness and mercy shall follow me all the days of my life: and I will dwell in the house of the LORD forever.

After this, I ask God to bless and awaken the herbs and thank them for their lives and make the request for the rue to remove negativity. Finalize your prayer and request with the word *Amen* (meaning: "So be it" or "The Truth").

Next, boil enough water in a pot to fill a spray bottle. When the water is ready, add the tablespoon of rue to it and remove the pot from the heat. Allow the rue to steep in the water for thirteen minutes. Then, immediately strain the rue and set it aside to later return it to the ground from whence it came, displaying respect for the herb. Let the Rue Water cool.

As with the other waters mentioned earlier, simply pour the Rue Water into a previously unused spray bottle. Starting from the crown of your head and working downward to your feet, spray yourself from top to bottom in a symbolic gesture of making something go away, while stating aloud with each spray that negativity will leave you and your aura is cleansed and protected. Then, take the herb outside, thank it, and respectfully place it on the ground.

Other Herbal Waters

There is an array of other marvelous herbs, roots, and minerals that can also rid a person or space of negative energies. A few more of the most popular herbs used to eradicate negative energies are given here. Later when we explore spiritual bathing, we'll discuss more details of these marvels.

* **Agrimony** (*Agrimonia eupatoria*): Widely used for protection and to banish both negative energies as well as negative spirits.

* **Hyssop** (*Hyssopus officinalis*): As popular as rue, hyssop is a purification herb.

★ **Rosemary** (*Rosemarinus officinalis*): A powerful herb used for cleansing and purifying negative vibrations.

Prepare the herb exactly as instructed for Rue Water. If desired, you can prepare an herbal water using more than one of the herbs listed above. Simply place two or more of the herbs in the pot of boiling water and continue with the usual steps.

Sulfur Soap

Sulfur (*sulphurium*), known in the magical practices by its folkloric name "brimstone," is used in both negative and positive spellwork. Some of its positive magical properties could purge unwanted emotions and clean a person's energy field.

I keep a bar of Sulfur Soap in my shower and bathe with it every morning and night. Because sulfur is a little harsh on the skin, some manufacturers of Sulfur Soap make it milder to avoid irritation. Nevertheless, ensure that you have no skin allergies or sensitivities to the soap before you do a full wash. Test its effect on a small area of your skin, preferably the inner wrist. Then immediately rinse it off and wait to see if there are any unfavorable effects.

If you show no adverse effects such as redness, swelling, itching, discoloration, or altered skin integrity, it ought to be safe to use. Simply bathe with this soap as you would with any other soap, but add in a spoken petition for your spiritual result. Tell the soap what you want to do: "Cleanse my energy fields." Then, rinse off and towel dry.

Rue Soap

As previously discussed, rue eradicates negative energies and has protective properties. Bathe with Rue Soap as you normally do with any soap, but also stating your petition aloud while bathing. A simple command could be: "Cleanse and protect my energy fields." Then, rinse off and towel dry.

Cleansing with an Egg

It is believed in many African Derivative Traditions (ADRs) that an egg will absorb the negativity from within us, if we roll it over our bodies. It is an ideal technique for removing minor attacks.

There are a couple of ways to perform this ritual. The first technique is to gently place the egg on top of your head then, slowly and carefully, roll it around and downward to your feet, while ensuring that it is rolled over all surfaces of the body.

The second technique is to gently rub it directly over the seven major chakras, or energy centers, that connect the spiritual self to the physical body. Start with the crown chakra and work your way down to the root chakra while stating your petition or command aloud each time:

* **Crown chakra**—at the crown of the head
* **Brow chakra**—between the eyebrows
* **Throat chakra**—within the throat
* **Heart chakra**—within the heart
* **Solar plexus chakra**—sits over the stomach, above the naval
* **Sacral chakra**—in the pelvis, near the sacrum
* **Root chakra**—at the base of the spine

Once the egg has consumed the undesirable energies, it must be deployed to remove the negativity from both you and your surroundings. My Aunt Isabel would smash the egg into the toilet, then flush, while screaming in Spanish that all negativity leave at once.

My mother, on the other hand, was a more patient soul. Prior to disposing of the egg in the toilet, down the drain, or even in a sewer, she first liked to see if the cleansing had worked. This was accomplished by breaking the egg into a glass of water, waiting twenty-four hours, and then examining the symbols made by the egg white and yolk. If the symbols were unfavorable, another egg cleansing was warranted. If two consecutive cleansings were unsuccessful, stronger modes of spiritual cleansings—like those we will explore later in this book—were implemented.

The Power of Crystals

Crystals have been an essential tool of magical practitioners for thousands of years. We know that crystals are mentioned in the Holy Bible countless times and have been utilized for innumerable purposes.

My faith in the power of crystals goes back to an incident that happened decades ago when I once visited a disreputable backyard dog breeder. The breeder had this beautifully angelic puppy who was filled with repulsive fleas and other infestations. However, I couldn't resist the way that she looked at me, so I purchased her.

After a veterinarian had rid her of the obvious problems, weeks later she developed more serious issues. Having spent more than $7,000 between five different veterinarians, I still had no firm diagnosis and she was dying. The last animal clinic arranged an intervention for me that included a couple of veterinarians and a small group of employees insisting that I have my beautiful girl put to sleep. I refused and opted for spellwork with crystals instead.

First I informed a double terminated (meaning a point at each end), clear crystal quartz about the problem—by placing it in both of my hands, gently bringing it to my mouth, and speaking my problem aloud—and asked for its help. The crystal was then placed directly on my puppy's belly, pleading for her disease to go away. I moved the crystal to another part of her belly, with the same plea. This tedious process was repeated numerous times to ensure that the crystal was in direct contact with every part of her belly.

Ultimately, the clear crystal consumed the disease, and it turned visibly black. My puppy was cured, regained optimal health within three weeks, and she lived to be eleven years old. The power of crystals is amazing!

All life contains spirit, and this includes plants and minerals. Crystals are minerals, and each of them hold energy, possess spirits, and—just like humans and animals—even have their own personalities.

Keep this in mind when selecting crystals. Hold your options in your hand, one by one, and feel if there are compatible or repelling energies. I cannot begin to count how many times a crystal didn't like me. Once a crystal disliked me so much that it literally jumped out of my hand! So when choosing a crystal, take the time to feel the type of energy being emitted. What you feel will be a warm positive feeling, no feeling at all, or repulsion. Only buy those that emit a warm positive feeling.

Love Is in the Earth: A Kaleidoscope of Crystals— Update, authorized by Melody, is a comprehensive resource on almost every crystal and stone known to humankind. It has been one of my personal go-to crystal books for decades. Melody discusses numerous functions of each individual crystal while providing a comprehensive list of crystals that cleanse the aura. However, for this chapter, we will list solely the most common and available crystals to remove negativity:

* **Amethyst** clears the aura and stabilizes it.

* **Ametrine** disperses negativity from the aura.

* **Andradite** clears the aura.

* **Aurichalcite** clears the aura while soothing it.

* **Boji stone** cleanses and charges the aura.

* **Citrine** clears and aligns the aura.

* **Fluorite (colorless)** clears and energizes the aura.

* **Jasper** cleanses the aura.

* **Quartz,** such as curved, faden, etc., will clean the aura.

* **Brown tourmaline** clears the aura.

Before use, all of these crystals except citrine must be cleansed. This can be done in various ways from simply smudging the crystal with the smoke of white sage or burying it in sea salt for twenty-four hours to elaborate two-day rituals that involve burying it in sea salt for twenty-four hours, rinsing with ice water, smudging with sage smoke, repeating the process, and then placing it outside to absorb the sun- and/or moonlight. All are effective techniques, so the choice is yours.

There are numerous techniques for cleansing the aura with crystals. The simplest method is to ask the crystal to assist in ridding your aura of negative energies. Then, as with the egg cleansing technique, rub each of the seven major chakras with the crystal while restating your petition. The crystal must be cleansed afterward.

Protecting the Aura from Minor Attacks

Once the aura is cleansed, it must be protected; otherwise it remains vulnerable to subsequent attacks. Think of it as being caught in a sudden rainstorm. The ground turns muddy, and you are forced to walk through it. Without the proper attire, you will be contaminated with mud. You return home as quickly as possible to bathe and rid yourself of the dirt and filth but then remember you must go out again. This time, you don a raincoat and boots to protect yourself against the mud. But what would happen without the protective apparel? Obviously, you would return home as filthy as you were the first time.

The same principles apply to spiritual cleansing and protection. Cleansing the aura can repair or minimize the damage caused by the negative stimuli, but it will not stop further attacks. People may still argue with or insult you; others will still hold on to prejudices or envy against you, while some will even hate you. Unfortunately, magical protection cannot control the thoughts or intentions of others. However, taking protective steps will serve as a deterrent to further incoming assaults while safeguarding your emotional and spiritual well-being when negative energies are directed toward you. As with the rainstorm, we cannot control it, but we can certainly minimize the potential damage to ourselves by wearing protective gear.

Please keep in mind that cleansing and protecting the aura ought to be performed on a regular basis. Sometimes we are not consciously aware of any attacks, such as malevolent people gossiping or talking against us while wishing us harm or even casting spells at us. These malicious thoughts and actions are energies that will ultimately find their way to you and affect your aura. As a result, they produce feelings of discomfort both emotionally and often physically.

Therefore, it is a good policy to always be consciously aware of your shield and its maintenance. My suggestions are to cleanse the aura at least weekly while providing daily protection boosters.

Condition Oils

Condition Oils are prepared oils that assist us with the status for which we seek aid. They are also known as dressing oils, conjure oils, anointing oils, ritual oils, etc. A quality condition oil will contain herbs and/or essential oils, have been prepared according to ancient documents, and/or have been prayed over by religious authorities.

There are several ways to properly anoint oneself with a condition oil for protection. Since some practitioners believe that negative energies will attach themselves to the back of the head and neck, while others believe that the energies will attack our chakras, two anointing methods will be described. Please note that it is traditional to work upward to draw protective energies to you.

The first method is to place oil in your hand, then, starting at the neck, rub the oil up to the crown of your head while stating your petition aloud. The second method is to anoint each of the seven major chakras with the oil, starting with the root chakra, then working your way up to the crown chakra, while stating your petition aloud each time.

Although there are many condition oils designed for protection, these are some of the most widely used:

- ★ **Blessing Oil** bestows either holy or divine strength.

- ★ **Eucalyptus Oil** provides strong protective properties and has a potent odor.

- ★ **Holy Oil** has either been prayed over by a religious authority or has been prepared according to ancient texts. It has a connection with God.

- ★ **Protection Oil** will contain the proper herbs and/ or essential oils that provide protection. There will be slight variations in label names, but all quality oils will do.

⋆ **Rue Oil** contains the herb that is one of the oldest
and most widely used plants for both protection
and ridding oneself from negative energies.

Always remember that once we bathe, we have also
washed away our protection oil. Therefore, it is a good
idea to immediately reapply the oil upon exiting the
shower or tub.

Protection Crystals

As previously discussed, crystals have spirits. Therefore, it
is essential to establish a respectful relationship with such
spirits. Treating your crystal with high regard will get you
the same in return, whereas treating it as an insignificant
object will get you nothing in return. In other words, you
will reap what you sow. My clients are always advised to
treat their mojo hands, herbs, minerals, roots, animal
curios, and crystals as if they are family.

Each individual crystal can perform many functions.
For instance, iron pyrite not only provides protection, but is
also a money-drawing stone! That's why you need to talk to
your crystal and ask it exactly what you wish it to do. If you
desire more than one role from it, ensure that your desires
are prioritized. Also, try not to ask too many favors at once
because, just like humans, the more that is asked of it, the
weaker the crystal will become.

Ensure that the crystal is cleansed prior to utilizing
it. You never know who has touched a stone, where it
has been, and what energies it may have accrued before
it came to you. Cleansing ought to be performed, at a
minimum, on a weekly basis. After it is clear, make your
request.

Your crystals can be worn as jewelry, carried in a clean
small bag worn close to the body, or carried within your

clothing, such as in pockets or undergarments. When not in use, store them in a comfortable environment, preferably wrapped in a natural cloth.

Some of the most easily attainable crystals utilized for protection include:

- ★ **Amber** protects our energies.
- ★ **Amethyst** is a powerful protection stone.
- ★ **Cat's-eye** protects the aura.
- ★ **Carnelian** protects against envy and resentment.
- ★ **Jade** protects from harm.
- ★ **Jet** is a powerful protection stone used in many spiritual practices. As an azabache, it is pinned to babies to protect them from bad energies and entities.
- ★ **Labradorite** acts as a shield to deflect unwanted energies.
- ★ **Obsidian** forms a shield against negativity.
- ★ **Pyrite** also forms a shield around the aura.
- ★ **Smoky quartz** protects against bad energies such as those that may result in depression.
- ★ **Tigereye** protects against people who wish you harm or perform curses on you.
- ★ **Black tourmaline** is a powerful protection crystal.
- ★ **Turquoise** protects and strengthens the aura.

Protection from the Harmful Energies of Mercury in Retrograde

Mercury in Retrograde is an event that occurs for around a three-week period, three to four times a year, which interferes with direct or technological channels of communication. It is a time when computers break down, phone calls will either be disrupted or discontinued, or there's miscommunication between people. The results are frustration, tension, and anger.

Many astrologers proclaim that those born with their sun, moon, or ascendant (rising) sign in Gemini or Virgo, which are ruled by Mercury, are likely to be more severely affected. Having my own rising sign in Virgo, I found this proclamation valid until I miraculously discovered a website called *Hibiscusmooncrystalacademy.com,* written by Hibiscus Moon. By simply placing the five crystals that she recommends into a yellow cloth bag and putting this in my undergarment, Mercury in Retrograde no longer affects me or my emotions!

* **Aquamarine** fosters clear communication.

* **Emerald** smooths communication.

* **Blue lace agate** improves communication.

* **Amazonite** harmonizes communication.

* **Fluorite (any color)** also improves communication.

The Protective Power of Amulets

The word *amulet,* arising from the Latin root *amuletum* meaning "an object that protects a person from trouble," was first introduced in the writings of Pliny the Elder in 77–79 CE. However, they had been utilized for centuries before this due to the powers they possess to protect the bearer by emitting specific defensive vibrations.

Amulets are employed by almost every culture around the world and exist in many varieties. Most amulets are worn by the bearer and may include gems, coins, pendants, rings, written words, and plant parts, such as roots.

Listed below are the most typical types of amulets.

* **Spiritual deities:** The image of a sacred deity is said to be infused with their powers.

* **Religious or spiritual symbolism:** Images such as a crucifix or any other sacred object that contains a representation of protection.

* **All-Seeing Eye (Lucky Eye, Anti-Evil-Eye):** To ward off the evil eye sent by another.

* **Hamsa Hand:** Believed by many Jews, Muslims, and Christians to ward off the evil eye.

* **Silver dimes:** If worn as an anklet, it's believed the wearer cannot be affected by any negative spells cast by being stepped over.

* **Pentagram of Solomon:** This symbol protects the wearer from curses and evil spirits.

* **Mirror charms:** Worn or pinned to your garment, with the reflective side facing away from your body, these deflect negative energies back to the sender.

* **Charms or jewelry containing protection crystals:** Protection crystals are also set in necklaces, bracelets, earring, rings, and other jewelry.

* **Lockets:** Written petitions, protection herbs, and/or other objects consecrated for protection may be kept inside the locket and worn as a pendant.

* **Master root:** This power-enhancing root protects both men and women. As an amulet, carry a whole root piece.

All amulets ought to be cleansed before wearing as we do not know who handled them before they came into our hands. Cleansing by lightly spraying with Florida Water, a little sea salt mixed with water, Holy Water, or whiskey will effectively rid them of any negative energies.

Follow up by anointing the amulet with a little Protection Oil while reciting Psalm 23 or by stating aloud that, by the power within you, the amulet is blessed. If a Protection Oil is not readily available, the prayer and/or blessing is sufficient.

Creative Visualization

An effective technique that has been employed for centuries is to visualize an energy field surrounding your entire body. You may see this called an Energy Shield, Psychic Protection Shield, or simply a Light Shield. As with other techniques, there are numerous variations ranging from self-induced deep meditative states to yoga practices.

However, when time is of the essence, simply go to a quiet place, take a few deep breaths to calm yourself down, and relax for a couple of minutes. Then, close your eyes and visualize a bright white light surrounding your feet. Visualize the light moving upward until your entire body is engulfed with it.

The light is sufficient; however, you may also wish to visualize protective symbols floating within the light. My preference is to picture tiny crucifixes, and sometimes I will also visualize Jesus Christ smiling at me.

If you employ this technique as directed, once you open your eyes you will actually feel the light surrounding you. Many of my friends use this technique as a daily ritual. Better safe than sorry!

Protection Prayers

Prayer places us in contact with the deity whom we wish to reach. It is a form of a rite or ritual just as spellcasting is.

Effective praying means knowing that you have been heard. In other words you must have faith that the communication took place. When we have doubts or pray without conviction, usually nothing will happen. If someone asks us for help in a robotic manner, we tend to ignore them because we sense a lack of sincerity in their pleas. But if they are humble, respectful, and ask with conviction, we will most likely assist them. The same is true when petitioning deities.

Psalm 91 is one of the most powerful prayers of protection in the Hebrew Bible as well as the Old Testament of the Christian Holy Bible:

PSALM 91

1 He that dwelleth in the secret place of the most High shall abide under the shadow of the Almighty.

2 I will say of the LORD, He is my refuge and my fortress: my God; in him will I trust.

3 Surely he shall deliver thee from the snare of the fowler, and from the noisome pestilence.

4 He shall cover thee with his feathers, and under his wings shalt thou trust: his truth shall be thy shield and buckler.

5 Thou shalt not be afraid for the terror by night; nor for the arrow that flieth by day;

6 Nor for the pestilence that walketh in darkness; nor for the destruction that wasteth at noonday.

7 A thousand shall fall at thy side, and ten thousand at thy right hand; but it shall not come nigh thee.

8 Only with thine eyes shalt thou behold and see the reward of the wicked.

9 Because thou hast made the LORD, which is my refuge, even the most High, thy habitation;

10 There shall no evil befall thee, neither shall any plague come nigh thy dwelling.

11 For he shall give his angels charge over thee, to keep thee in all thy ways.

12 They shall bear thee up in their hands, lest thou dash thy foot against a stone.

13 Thou shalt tread upon the lion and adder: the young lion and the dragon shalt thou trample under feet.

14 Because he hath set his love upon me, therefore will I deliver him: I will set him on high, because he hath known my name.

15 He shall call upon me, and I will answer him: I will be with him in trouble; I will deliver him and honor him.

16 With long life will I satisfy him and shew him my salvation.

Remember to pray aloud and, before ending any prayer with the closing of "Amen," make your petition. Be respectful, be humble, and show gratitude. Most importantly, have faith that your prayer is being heard.

2

Negative Energies in the Home

Energies in the home behave in the same manner as dust. Think about how dust distributes itself: some particles scatter around, while others gather to make larger piles. Logically, if you don't cleanse away the dust and dirt, the accumulation accelerates and becomes an insult to both sight and smell. Sometimes, the insult is so drastic that it impairs our ability to move freely because we fear contamination.

Just as dust circulates all over the home, so do the different types of energies. We've all walked into other people's homes and felt a range of good, neutral, uncomfortable, and bad feelings. For instance, when people have recently argued, we can actually feel the ambiance of that tension, which makes us yearn to leave as soon as possible. On the flip side, if the energies are positive, we sometimes overstay our welcome! This is because our own energy fields are capable of sensing other energies and react accordingly.

Let's look at a particular example of living in a dirty home and how it will eventually contaminate both your clothing and your body. I have three German Shepherd dogs that perpetually shed their coats. Neglecting to vacuum every day would allow their hair to fly all over the house and eventually mess up my clothing and my food, resulting in emotional discomfort. Eventually, the hair could enter my nasal passageways and obstruct my sense of smell and breathing, which would be a direct attack on my physiological well-being. Similar principles apply to living with unfavorable energies. Think of the negative particles as you would the dog hair: when the energy particles scatter, they will attach themselves to fixtures or accumulate in particular areas of your home, usually lurking alongside the clutter and dust. These energies behave as a vacuum, bringing in more of the same because "like begets like."

Without aura cleansing and protection, even minor annoyances will attract negative energies that will ultimately enter your home. We've all had days of resistance that affect our psychological well-being, such as:

* ★ Having a bad day at work

* ★ Traffic backups

* ★ Lack of cooperation from others

* ★ Delay or resistance in plans

* ★ Minor health problems such as headaches

When we get home, we eventually recover. However, even after our personal recovery, such negative energies do not just suddenly disappear. They instead disperse and remain somewhere in your home, hiding and accumulating more of the same.

Negative energies are also introduced into your home in other ways. Consider your visitors or service people. Haven't you ever interacted with someone and felt uncomfortable around them yet you could not identify the problem because their behaviors seemed to be kind and gentle? Or maybe you just didn't like the person but couldn't identify the source of the dislike. They were probably good people but, unfortunately, carrying negative energies that could be dispersed in your home. Perhaps they were not taking care of their own auras and so were carrying around a lot of spiritual dirt. If we go back to the dog hair analogy, a dog that doesn't have regular baths will have more hair (negative energy) to shed where we don't want it.

Another situation that might shed negative energy in your personal space might be if a friend visits needing a lending ear or a helping hand in problem-solving. Even if this is not something that makes you feel uncomfortable, it could leave a residue of negative energies.

Also consider the type of energies prior tenants or owners of your home may have introduced into the dwelling. Did they argue? Were there tensions? Were there psychological or physiological illnesses? Be mindful of what may have been left behind.

With the many possibilities around for home contamination, a spiritual house cleansing can safeguard your well-being. There are other advantages too: the air will feel "lighter"; it will seem easier to take deep breaths; and you'll sleep better too!

Cleansing, Blessing, and Protecting the Home for the First Time

Step 1. Spiritual Cleaning

Within the multitudes of spiritual and religious traditions, there are many customs and techniques available to choose from in order to rid your dwelling of negativity.

For instance, in the Hoodoo tradition, pine is considered to be not only a spiritual cleanser but also an ingredient used for money drawing. The brand Pine-Sol is sometimes used as a spiritual cleanser because its main ingredient is pine. There are other brands of cleansers that also claim to contain pine, but please read the labels to ensure that they do not contain an artificial pine substitute, which is unacceptable. Optionally, you may add a single drop of essential oil of pine to a cup of pure castile liquid soap and mix well. When you are ready to use it, add about one-quarter of the soap to a bucket of water.

Salt will do anything that you want it to do. I remember when my mother didn't have a means of transportation to the store but needed to get rid of what she called "bad luck." She would simply dissolve a few tablespoons of salt in a bucket of water and then mop the floor while commanding all bad luck to leave her house immediately.

Making a strong tea out of protection herbs such as rue, rosemary, or agrimony, then mixing it with pure liquid castile soap for a cleanser will also remove negativity. If you are fortunate to have the essential oils of the aforementioned, that's even better! Remember to only add one drop of the oil in one-quarter cup of pure castile soap, then follow the instructions given for the pine cleanser.

In the Catholic tradition, it is believed that a few drops of Holy Water added to any body of water will turn the rest of that water into Holy Water. Pour about a quarter cup of Holy Water into your clean bucket of water.

Ammonia will get rid of anything harmful; however, it can also eliminate good entities. Many decades ago, I brought a gallon of unopened ammonia into my godfather's house of Santería. It was one of only three times that he ever lost his temper with me. He stated—or, to be more exact, *screamed*—that ammonia would drive away the orishas, the deities of Santería, from his house! Additionally, ammonia is harmful to many surfaces. Therefore, the instructions for use will be explored in more detail later in this book.

My preferred cleanser is Chinese Wash, a spiritual cleaning agent typically utilized by Hoodoo practitioners for spiritual house cleansing, purification, and other rites. Its odor is pleasant and uplifting. Among its key ingredients is Van Van Oil, which contains lemongrass in the form of an herb or essential oil, which removes negativity and brings forth good luck. Chinese Wash is available for purchase at most shops that sell magical supplies, or you can make your own. My personal recipe has brought great success to both myself and my clients.

Miss Aida's Chinese Wash Recipe

One 32-ounce bottle of Murphy Oil Soap

One 1/2-ounce bottle of quality Van Van Oil

2 ounces of liquid pure castile soap (to dilute the Murphy Oil Soap)

One frankincense incense tear (to enhance the power of the formula)

1 tablespoon of lemongrass

13 new broom straws (aids in spiritual cleansings)

A little bit of your saliva

Remove about three ounces of Murphy Oil Soap from the bottle to make room then add the Van Van Oil and castile soap to the bottle. Agitate the bottle to disperse the liquids. Add the frankincense tear, followed by the lemongrass, then the broom straws. Replace the cap and gently shake the bottle. Once it appears that the lemongrass has been dispersed, remove the cap. Place your mouth close to the lip of the bottle and recite Psalm 23. Then respectfully release a little of your saliva into the bottle to activate or charge the ingredients. Your Chinese Wash is now ready for use.

Use about one-quarter cup of Chinese Wash per bucket of water. A new mop is preferable to wash the floor, but a clean mop will suffice. You will also need clean rags to wipe down walls and other surfaces.

House Cleansing Ritual

It is a typical Hoodoo cleansing ritual to begin your house washing at the top level of your dwelling and working downward. The cleansers I have listed are safe enough to use on walls, and therefore, do include wall washing with the first-time cleansing. It does not matter if you wash the walls or if others do it for you.

As you work from room to room, start by washing the walls. Then, work downward and pay special attention to cleaning any windows, windowsills, doors, and thresholds. If this is an empty house, the last surface to clean is the floor before going to the next room. Chinese Wash and cleansers with a castile liquid soap base can also be used in a carpet shampooer or, if one is not available, simply place a diluted mixture of one part cleanser to ten parts of water in a spray bottle, then lightly spray the carpets.

If this is an occupied home, before cleaning the floor be sure to clean the other fixtures in the room. The Murphy Oil Soap in the recipe provided for Chinese Wash makes the wash safe to use on wood furniture. However, if you are using a store-bought Chinese Wash, avoid the wood because the ingredients could be harmful to the furniture.

If there is clutter in the home, remember that negative energies hide in clutter. Prior to rearranging the disorder and scattering these energies, pour Florida Water in

a spray bottle and lightly spray the clutter to first eradicate these particles. It is then safe to move or rearrange
what was clutter and introduce organization and space.
Remember that the floor is the last surface to wash before
moving on to the next room.

As you work from room to room, recite aloud any
prayer that feels comfortable and relates to purification
or house blessings. My favorite prayer for purification is
Psalm 84.

PSALM 84

1 How amiable are thy tabernacles, O Lord of hosts!

*2 My soul longeth, yea, even fainteth for the courts
of the Lord: my heart and my flesh crieth out for the
living God.*

*3 Yea, the sparrow hath found an house, and the
swallow a nest for herself, where she may lay her
young, even thine altars, O Lord of hosts, my King,
and my God.*

*4 Blessed are they that dwell in thy house: they will be
still praising thee. Selah.*

*5 Blessed is the man whose strength is in thee; in
whose heart are the ways of them.*

*6 Who passing through the valley of Baca make it a
well; the rain also filleth the pools.*

*7 They go from strength to strength, every one of them
in Zion appeareth before God.*

*8 O Lord God of hosts, hear my prayer: give ear, O
God of Jacob. Selah.*

9 Behold, O God our shield, and look upon the face of thine anointed.

10 For a day in thy courts is better than a thousand. I had rather be a doorkeeper in the house of my God, than to dwell in the tents of wickedness.

11 For the Lord God is a sun and shield: the Lord will give grace and glory: no good thing will he withhold from them that walk uprightly.

12 O Lord of hosts, blessed is the man that trusteth in thee.

As with all prayers, state or ask your petition prior to ending your prayer with the word *Amen.* An example of what you might say for house cleansing is "God, please remove all negativity from my home."

Each time the pail of soapy water becomes dirty, some practitioners will throw it out the front door. Although this is an old practice, my preferred method is to pour it down the toilet to keep the negativity as far away from you and your home as possible. As you do so, state aloud that all negativity will leave both you and your home immediately. Refill your bucket with warm water and your wash. Continue your cleansing ritual room by room, until all the floors and walls have been cleansed and the dirty water has been disposed.

It is customary in some households to follow up by returning to each room and lightly spritzing Florida Water up into the air, in a clockwise fashion. Keep in mind that Florida Water has an alcohol base, and alcohol acts as a solvent that can destroy materials by liquifying them. Therefore, avoid direct contact with any materials that can be harmed, such as wood, leather, and other susceptible fabrics or textiles.

Now that your dwelling has been cleansed of negative energies, you will be able to feel a substantial difference. Some people report that after a cleansing, they no longer have a "binding" feeling and instead have a sense of freedom. Others say that there are feelings of relaxation and happiness, while some clients have simply shared: "I can't explain it, but it just feels wonderful!"

Hopefully, these favorable sensations will inspire you to move on to your next steps for bringing in positive energies, protecting your home from any future negative contamination, and maintaining the protection that has been established.

Step 2. Blessing Your Home (Optional)

Once the home is cleansed, the next step is to bless your dwelling in order to invite the positive energies of a spiritual deity. In most religious practices, there is a church leader, or an appointee, who will perform a house blessing for you. Different faiths have different traditions; therefore, it is prudent to first consult your spiritual or religious leader.

In most Christian faiths, the house blessing consists of a pastor, priest, or deacon walking from room to room sprinkling Holy Water and/or anointing areas of your home with Holy Oil, while reciting prayers to bring forth the grace of God in your home. Although a house blessing from a professional leader is ideal, sometimes there are constraining factors preventing a home visit such as distance, time constraints, or insufficient staffing, which forces the leaders to prioritize the needs of their followers or congregation. Therefore, it is acceptable to perform you own home blessing.

The most common practice is to select a room to begin the house blessing ritual, preferably the same room where the cleansing began, while following the same order of direction as the cleansing. Sprinkle Holy Water around the room, in a clockwise fashion, while reciting a short prayer, asking for peace, love, harmony, or the grace of God. The prayer may be in your own words or you may recite a formal one such as Proverbs 24:3–4:

By wisdom a house is built,
and through understanding it is established;
through knowledge its rooms are filled
with rare and beautiful treasures.

You may also anoint your doors and windows with Holy Oil. Drawing a religious or spiritual symbol on the doors with eggshell powder, called *cascarilla*, is also common.

Step 3. Protecting Your Home

Although a complete home cleansing ought to be performed at least twice a year, there are methods to protect the home from unwanted energies entering between those cleanings. Protection measures are also to be performed immediately after the cleaning or the blessing if you had opted for a house blessing. Some people will spiritually clean a room, bless it, protect it, and then move on to the next room. The choice is yours; both options are equally effective.

While negative energies enter the home by being carried in by people, they can also enter through doorways, windows, or other openings from the outside world. Therefore, we must pay special attention to these specific areas.

Making straight lines with a protective agent across door thresholds, windowsills, and near other entrances such as fireplaces acts as both a barrier and deterrent for unwanted energies. Some of the most commonly used protection agents against harmful energies include the following:

* **Black salt** is used in negative spells but also works to drive away evil.

* **Holy Oil** has a connection with God.

* **Protection Oil** keeps away harmful energies.

* **Rue Oil** is used for protection and eliminating harmful energies.

* **Sea salt** will do anything that you will it to and also drives away negativity.

* **Sulfur** drives away any unwanted negativity and kills jinxes.

Remember that drains, such as those of sinks, bathtubs, showers, and toilets are also openings to and from the outside world. Additionally, bathrooms are notorious for harboring harmful germs, which will attract harmful energies. Spraying these areas with Florida Water will cleanse the spaces from negativity. Florida Water is also produced in an aerosol formula but a spray bottle is just as effective.

Guarding Doors and Windows

Having a purifying agent near the entrances of your doors assists in decontaminating what may attempt to enter the home. Both camphor and Florida Water are purifying agents. Many negative entities are repulsed by the odor of camphor. Having a votive cup filled with Florida Water and one square of camphor is an excellent way to maintain purification. Florida Water does evaporate rapidly, so it has to be monitored for frequent refills. However, a fellow conjure worker once taught me a less labor-intensive technique: The main ingredient of Vicks Vaporub, the brand-name cough suppressant and topical analgesic, is camphor. There are also other name brands with the same amount of camphor that can be purchased at a reduced price. Simply remove the lid and place the open jar near the entrances of your home for purification purposes and replace this with a new jar when the odor has dissipated. If you are a pet owner, please ensure that your fur-babies maintain their distance from either the votive cup or the jar.

A simple reversing rite to avert and return any bad energies aimed toward you can be carried out so inexpensively with mirrors. With the reflective side facing outward, place mirrors on or near windows and on the outside of doors. Feng shui practitioners have a similar custom using *bagua* mirrors.

A bell hung on the door protects the home not only from evil spirits but also from malicious intent. Doorknob bells readily perform this function and are easy to find on sale, especially during the Christmas season. Keeping or removing any Christmas decorations attached to them is optional; this ornamentation does not defeat their purpose or task.

Salt drives away negativity. Open bags of salt, or even rock salt, can be placed outside your doors for protection. I have seen hundreds of spiritual stores do this to protect their business.

Red brick dust is a modern version of the ancient red ocher clay used for rites. Sprinkling red brick dust across the doorstep of your home provides protection.

Basil is considered a sacred herb in many cultures and performs numerous functions including protection. It is

believed that evil cannot step where basil has been. Sprinkling dried basil leaves across the doorstep will provide
safety from negative energies. Alternatively, make a wash
to scrub the doorstep. Boil water and basil, then strain the
fluid into a bucket of water. Mop across the doorstep with
this wash. Respectfully dispose of the boiled basil by placing it outside on the ground.

Catholic homeowners sometimes have Holy Water
fonts on the walls immediately upon entering the home.
This provides a dual function: to keep the blessings of God
within the home and to bless themselves with the water
upon arriving. The font is a little concave bowl, usually
attached to ornate images of deities; however, the imagery is not necessary. Alternatively, a small votive cup filled
with Holy Water can be placed on a structure close to your
entranceway. Either pour the Holy Water directly into the
cup or font, or place a piece of a new sponge into it and
then fill it with water. Because of evaporation, refills will
be required on a regular basis.

Plants Offering Protection Properties

Many household plants also provide protection to the
home. These plants include:

- ★ Cacti
- ★ Ferns
- ★ Ivy
- ★ Palms

Upon bringing the plant home, welcome it in a soft loving
voice. Introduce yourself to it as well as tell it that this is its
new home. Ask the plant to provide protection to its new
dwelling. Take good care of your new house member, and
it will take good care of you!

Amulets, Talismans, and Curios to Hang over Your Entranceways

As discussed earlier, amulets are objects that protect a person from trouble, are employed by almost every culture around the world, and exist in an array of types. A talisman is also a magical object, usually inscribed with magical codes, used to avert evil and bring good luck. A curio is basically an object considered novel, rare, or out of the ordinary—such as a plant root or animal body part—that has a specific meaning to the owner. Due to their vibrational properties, they will also protect a home or any area where they are placed. The following items are the most common types of protection amulets, talisman, and curios seen at entranceways. However, it is most certainly acceptable to utilize the same amulets discussed for keeping on your person for entranceway protection.

* **St. Benedict medal:** St. Benedict of Nursia/Norcia, the patron saint of Europe, is venerated in the Catholic, Eastern Orthodox, and Anglican Communion, and other churches. He performed an array of miracles during his lifetime including restoring life to a dead teenager, walking on water, and warfare with the Devil and his temptations. His powerful medal contains the symbolism, depicted in code, to combat spiritual and physical dangers and to ward off evil. I have this medal over every door in my house, as well as every window, so that no spiritual danger may enter my home. However, one medal over the main entryway will suffice.

* **St. Michael the Archangel medal:** Venerated in Judaism, Christianity, and Islam, St. Michael is a warrior saint who battles for righteousness in the name of God. There are various biblical accounts

of his victories over evil and injustice. He is often depicted conquering the Devil in war. Medals of St. Michael can be placed over your entrances as a potent defense against evil.

★ **Mezuzah:** In all the Jewish homes I have visited, there has always been a mezuzah, meaning "door-post" in Hebrew, affixed to the outside of the door on the entrance side. These are cases containing Hebrew verses from the Torah. I have been told that their primary purpose is to establish a home that follows the Jewish law, but additionally, they direct the Spirit of God to the home and provide protection.

★ **Star of David:** Also known as the "Shield of David" or the "Magen David," this is a hexagram-shaped star, identified as the divine protection of King David. In Jewish folk magic, it is a strong protection symbol.

★ **Crucifix:** This is a depiction of Jesus on the cross. In Catholic beliefs, it is a powerful symbol to ward off evil. Widely implemented in Rite of Exorcism, exorcists share that its use is one of the most effective means to oppose the Devil. Other Christian denominations may also utilize either the crucifix or the symbol of the cross for protection, and these can be found at the entranceways of devout Christian homes.

★ **Pentagram and pentacle:** Sometimes these two terms are used interchangeably, but that is incorrect. In Wiccan and other Neopagan traditions, a pentagram is usually, but not always, portrayed as a five-pointed star. The pentacle, on the other hand, is a pentagram within a circle. The pentagram has magical symbolic meanings, and often it is also inscribed with magical protection symbols. I have frequently seen pentacles displayed at the entrances of spiritual stores.

* **Devil's pod (bat nut, ling nut, bull nut):** This looks to me like the head of the Devil! However, it is a dried seedpod that's widely and successfully used by Hoodoo practitioners to ward off evil, and you'll typically find these hung over a main doorway.

Step 4. Maintaining Protection and Positive Energies in the Home

If you have spiritually cleaned your home, blessed it, then positioned protection measures, any feelings of restraint and discomfort should have dissipated. Now your home should seem peaceful, harmonious, and welcoming.

However, in time negative energies will return just as dirt finds its way back into an unsoiled home. Unfortunately, it's virtually unavoidable. All of us will ultimately experience bad days at work, family disagreements, disputes with others, illnesses and/or frustrations, and so on, and we bring that negativity home or we experience these stressors within our dwelling. Additionally, other folks may disperse their negative particles when they visit. Therefore, we try to maintain spiritual cleanliness just as we try to maintain a spotless household: by avoiding buildup and growth.

Immediate cleanup is the ultimate preventative against buildup. How do we know when a maintenance cleansing is needed? My philosophy is: "When in doubt, clean it out!" Here are a few tactics to eradicate the early arrival of unwanted energies:

* **White sage** (*Salvia apiana*): Also known as "sacred sage," this shrub is native to the United States and

Mexico. Many Native American tribes burn these sacred leaves for spiritual cleansing in a ceremony called "smudging," a successful practice adopted by Neopaganism and other spiritual traditions. White sage is available in both loose-leaf form and bundles called "smudge sticks." A Native American shaman once taught me to place the leaves in an abalone shell, light them with a match, snuff out any fire, then walk around the dwelling in a clockwise fashion (although several witches I know will walk in a counterclockwise fashion, effecting a banishing) while dispersing the smoke with a feather. A smudge stick is easier and does not require a container for the leaves. Either way, state aloud that negativity will leave your home while you are smudging.

* **Incense:** Incense has been used in ritual practices since the ancient times. Even the Holy Bible advises us to do so in verses from such places as 2 Chronicles, Exodus 30–31, and so forth. It is said that incense carries messages directly to the spirit world. Numerous practitioners believe that because spirits are attracted to both the smoke of incense as well as its odor, using it facilitates expeditious assistance. Conversely, if we are attempting to eradicate a spiritual entity, there are properties in certain incenses that make the unwanted energies or visitors vulnerable to our demands. Always ensure that you state your commands aloud while burning. Incense can be easily made at home or purchased. Commercial incense is sold in many forms including:

  * **Natural resins:** The hardened sap of trees and burned on charcoal

- **Wood chips:** Burned on charcoal
- **Joss sticks:** The long slender self-lighting sticks seen most frequently, which burn quickly
- **Cones:** Also self-lighting and placed on a holder
- **Powders:** These are also self-lighting and ought to be placed on a censer. However, I personally prefer to place this type of incense on a hot charcoal disk that I put in the censer and also light the top portion of the incense once it's in the charcoal disc. This technique causes the incense to burn evenly.

Be aware that cut-rate or bargain brands are usually imitations. Instead, seek brands that contain the authentic ingredients such as herbs and/or condition oils. Resins and wood chips must be genuine.

Look for label names that talk about Banishing, Jinx Killer, Uncrossing, or other categorizations for the removal of unwanted energies.

Lighting a Charcoal Disc

Charcoal discs have both a concave—hollowed or rounded inward like the inside of a bowl—and a convex—curved or rounded outward—surface. With metal prongs, grasp the charcoal disc and light the concave surface, allowing it to sparkle for a few minutes. Then, place the convex side of the disc on the censer. Once the disc has turned gray, it is ready to accept the incense.

Homemade Incenses

Making your own incense is pretty easy: just add the desired condition oil, such as Banishing, Jinx Removal, Uncrossing, etc., and/or the appropriate powdered herb into a self-lighting unscented black incense powder. Place this on the lit charcoal disc that is inside a censer and also light the top of the incense with a match or lighter.

Another option is to simply crush dried herbs with purification properties and place them on your lit charcoal disc. Crushing dried herbs can be accomplished by just clasping them in your hand, or for a finer texture, use a mortar and pestle. If you'd like a powdered texture, a miniature blender or food grinder is a faster and more efficient method to accomplish this.

Here is a list of a few of the most commonly employed tools for purification.

* **Herbs used as incense to cleanse and purify:**

    * **Agrimony** (*Agrimonia eupatoria*): Widely used for protection and to banish both negative energies as well as negative spirits.

    * **Asafoetida** (*Ferula foetida, Narthex asafoetida*): Also called "Devil's Dung," this is used in both banishing formulas and rituals. Another of its properties is to repel evil.

    * **Eucalyptus** (*Eucalyptus globulus, Eucalyptus spp.*): Used for eradicating evil energies.

    * **Hyssop** (*Hyssopus officinalis*): A purification herb.

    * **Rosemary** (*Rosemarinus officinalis*): Used for cleansing and purifying negativity.

* **Holy Water:** Can be poured into a spray bottle or dispersed by sprinkling it from your hand while walking around the house stating you petition aloud.

* **Holy Water and sugar:** An old Hoodoo tradition taught to me by elders is to place about one-quarter teaspoon of sugar into a cup of Holy Water

and mix. Next, gently sprinkle the mixture around the house to summon both the blessings of God and to also bring forth sweet energies. This formula is also used to calm down, or to induce tranquility, within an angry household.

* **Florida Water:** Pour into a spray bottle and walk around the home lightly spritzing into the air to purify the house. Do not spray directly on wood or textiles, such as leather, that are susceptible to its alcohol base.

* **Oil burners:** By placing the corresponding condition oil or diluted essential oil into an electric or candle-charged oil burner, the cleansing properties will be dispersed into the area where it is placed, but not throughout the entire home. Therefore, this method is costlier because more than one oil burner is needed.

* **Candles:** Prepared candles can be purchased at almost all spiritual shops and the labels will describe the condition for which they are used. Other options are to purchase a plain white candle and anoint it with a condition oil or pure olive oil, then roll it in a crushed herb used for purification. Unfortunately, just as with the oil burners, a quick house purification would require a candle for each room.

For everyday negative encounters, the rituals shared in these first chapters are more than sufficient to maintain spiritual harmony. Unfortunately, there are much severer conditions. Next we will explore a harsher form of negativity: the unforeseen visitors we inadvertently welcome into our homes . . .

3

Encountering Attached, Possessed, and Bewitched Objects

Energy Attachment to Objects

As previously discussed in chapter 2, we all emit particles of energy, just as a dog will shed its fur. These energies attach themselves to anything that will accept them, most commonly objects. Then, these objects will absorb the particles while continuing to accumulate more and more. Ultimately, if a vast amount of energy has been absorbed, the object will, in turn, discharge those very particles as vibrations. We can compare this to adding more fuel to a fire causing the fire to radiate more heat. With interactions, these discharged energies may attach to our own auras.

An object closest to a person or an object to which the person has established a personal bond will absorb the greatest amount of energies from that person's emotions, thoughts, moods, actions, and memories. In my career,

I have found that the most common objects with the highest amount of energies are jewelry, clothing, photographs, pillows, hobby tools, working tools, produced crafts such as artwork or knitted or crocheted items, favorite chairs, and mattresses. However, any object close to a person could accumulate energies, so it is impossible to concretely specify the objects containing attachments.

Haven't we all had at least one encounter with an object that has made us feel happy, depressed, angry, bitter, or other emotions that are not normal? What about those objects that we label as "lucky"? Many people cannot engage in any risk-taking activities without their "lucky shoes," "lucky coin," etc. This is because positive energies, or energies of achievement, are attached to that specific object and we are drawn to anything that makes us feel good. Conversely, we avoid objects that affect us in the opposite way. We might label them as being "bad luck," but the truth is that there are negative energies attached to the object.

If an emotion is extremely powerful, even handling the object only once will transmit many of those emotional particles directly to it. For instance, a murder weapon will have strong negative attachments absorbed from the anger of the perpetrator as well as the fear from the victim. Both powerful emotions attach to the weapon.

Unfortunately, because objects have a relatively long life span, the energies attached to them can linger indefinitely—even long after the person who imprinted them has died. Then, we sometimes inadvertently purchase these objects at garage sales, flea markets, estate sales, second-hand shops, consignment shops, auctions, etc. Other times, we may inherit an attached object or have been unlucky enough to have been given one as a gift.

Long after my husband passed away, I met a handsome, easy-going, debonair, well-cultured millionaire. He was the type of man that any woman would want as a permanent mate. I certainly did. So why didn't we marry? A stone was the cause of our breakup.

On September 11, 2001, two airplanes crashed into the Twin Towers in New York City, resulting in the deaths of 2,996 people with at least 6,000 others injured.

According to Wikipedia, it was the deadliest terrorist attack in human history. Unfortunately, my rich new boyfriend gifted me with a stone from the debris of that attack. I politely thanked him and put it aside on my table. I knew of the devastating energies of profound fear and traumatic death that this stone had absorbed. But I didn't want to hurt his feelings, so I graciously accepted it, while quietly planning to ritually dispose of it upon his return to New York.

However, that stone emitted profuse amounts of negative vibrations that affected everybody in my home. There were constant screaming, arguments, confusion, and feelings of profound desperation: emotions that I have never experienced in my life. Even my mother, normally an easygoing woman, joined the proverbial combat zone. Harsh words were exchanged, and he was eventually asked to leave my home. We never spoke again. To this day, I have no idea what caused the arguments, but the trauma of the event remains in my memory bank.

The following day, I had to dispose of the stone. It had absorbed and radiated so much negative energy that I didn't even wish to attempt a spiritual cleansing for it. Moreover, I had no intention of keeping that stone as it would have been a constant reminder of that horrid day and what my fellow human beings had sustained. Instead, I took it to a cemetery, far from the other graves, and recited prayers over it. Then, I buried it. When I got back home, both my mother and I ritually cleansed the house and then ourselves, and life returned to normal.

Even new objects could have energy attachments. For instance, in my practice I always spray my brand-new wrapped candles with either Florida Water or Sea Salt Water prior to working with them. My mind-set is that I don't know who has handled the candles prior to shipment. Anybody handling my candle could have had a recent horrific personal ordeal or even worse. Would a candle being used for love work have a successful outcome if it was handled by someone emitting negative energies into it? I just don't know, and it's better to be safe than sorry!

Obviously, not all objects have energy attachments, but it is a good policy to trust your gut prior to purchasing anything. The art of psychometry is the ability to see relevant associations with an object and its history by handling it. Although there are expert diviners capable of relaying detailed information, the simpler form is to take the time to hold it and see how or what you feel. If there are thoughts of a place or event, there might be an energy attachment. If there are negative feelings, do not buy it!

If the object is already in your possession, attempt a spiritual cleansing on it. Here are the most popular practices, but please first ensure that the object cannot be damaged by the spiritual cleansing agents you plan to use:

- ★ **Soak it in Florida Water.** If it is a larger object, spray it.

- ★ **Soak it in Sea Salt Water.** If it is a larger object, spray it.

- ★ **Soak it in Holy Water.** If it is a larger object, spray it.

- ★ **Soak it in ammonia.** If it is a larger object, spray it.

- ★ **Boil and freeze it.** An old Celtic practitioner once taught me to boil an object for thirteen minutes in water that contains a little sea salt. Then remove

it from the boiling water and place it in ice-cold
water for thirteen more minutes.

* ★ **Utilize the rinse cycle for clothing.** Place clothing
  in the washing machine, as one would normally do.
  However, during the rinse cycle, add Florida Water,
  Holy Water, or Sea Salt Water to the rinse cycle.

Possessed Objects

My Story: The Possessed Stones

The Encounter

Thirty years ago, my husband and I had planned a trip to
Cancún, Mexico. A witch acquaintance of mine urged me
to visit the nearby city of Chichen Itza, in the Mexican state
of Yucatán, while I was there. He said that the temple atop
the great pyramid El Castillo (also known as the Temple of
Kukulkan) contained "power stones." However, he did not
clearly define the word *power*. Nevertheless, my imagination got the best of me, and I just assumed that the stones
would give me more magical power, while failing to realize
that if something seems too good to be true, then it is . . .

During our trip to Mexico, my husband relaxed in
Cancún while I caught a local airplane, with careless pilots,
to Chichen Itza. Seeing the pyramid for the first time was
shocking! The pyramid, both steep and seventy-nine feet
high from the ground to the temple entrance was intimidating for someone like me who suffers from a condition called
basophobia, or the fear of falling. Although the thought of
getting to the temple was excruciating, my desire for the
notorious "power stones" prevailed. And so I climbed . . .

Once inside the temple, I looked directly at a bright
light, containing a blue hue, while it took the form of an

unidentified being. I heard his voice and he seemed nice. Others could see the light but not the form that it took, obviously visible only to me. Interestingly, nobody could define what this light was or its source. He was a spiritual entity.

After grabbing three stones from the floor—those closest to the entity—there was a nagging feeling that I was doing something wrong. But greed got the best of me for the "power" these stones had to offer. So I said goodbye to that bright light and left.

The repercussions for taking what wasn't mine started immediately as this basophobic climbed down the pyramid. Due to its steepness, the fear of falling consumed me, and ultimately, three employees had to help me down. Once on the ground I vowed never to climb another pyramid—especially that one!

The stones remained in my purse until we returned home. Once there, I placed one stone in my brassiere with the intent of always keeping it close to my person as one would with a mojo bag. Another stone went to my best friend Dru, and the last one was placed in a clay doll-baby.

For the first week, the stone that was on my person seemed dormant, but my best friend had disposed of her stone in the river within four days, professing that she felt it emitting negativity. I vehemently disagreed with her and told her that she was overreacting.

The Seduction

Ten days later, the stone placed inside the doll-baby made the person for whom the effigy was created a virtual slave to my commands. It was incredible! I became even more convinced that the purpose of the "power stones" was indeed to increase magical powers. However, believing that the stones had more to offer, I could not keep the last stone away from my body and cared for it as if it were a part of me and my daily routine. Pockets were even sewn into the inside of all of my pajamas in order to sleep with it.

Two weeks later, I had a strange dream involving a handicapped rabbi who was at the wrong wedding, and I helped him to find the correct one. Once I woke up, the dream seemed to be preposterous because as a Catholic, I had never personally known a rabbi. However, the dream was different than others I had had because all the events were mapped out sequentially and in great detail.

Later that day, my husband announced that he had forgotten to inform me that we had been invited to an associate's wedding reception, taking place that very evening. His perpetual absentmindedness was infuriating as well as embarrassing because we didn't have a wedding gift ready. Nevertheless, we attended the reception and sat at our assigned seats. The man next to me looked familiar. Within a few seconds, I saw his yarmulke and realized who he was.

I immediately asked him if he was a rabbi. He responded that he was indeed and had presided over his daughter's wedding. However, he didn't recognize anyone in this reception room. He was in the wrong area, and after having asked for names, I searched for, and found, the correct room. Upon returning to him—knowing from my dream that he was handicapped—I assisted him to the correct banquet hall. The sequence of events materialized exactly as in my dream.

Was it shocking? Of course! Now my greed prevailed—I believed that I could win the lottery and move on to bigger and better things! Right? Wrong!

The Consequences

Night after night, my dreams consisted only of useless forthcoming events for the following day. The dreams did not offer any value to me or to my loved ones, nor did they assist me with my psychic readings. Every night, I feared sleeping but refused to part with my stone—I just couldn't do it.

About five weeks later, the voice of the entity I had heard at the temple began to speak to me in my dreams. He wished to discuss profound scientific and esoteric matters, but his voice would awaken me, causing me to lose sleep. During the day, I was an emotional wreck from my lack of sleep and became dysfunctional. Every night, he insisted on conversations that were beyond my level of comprehension or interests.

Then he started speaking to me in the daytime. His demands for my attention were all-consuming. Although I begged him to leave me alone, he refused, so I tried my very best to ignore him. He became more persistent, making me feel as if I were losing my mind and punishing me for resisting him.

My first punishment came from the doll-baby that encased one of the stones. The person had a massive heart attack, professing that when it was occurring, he saw my face. The second punishment was strange phone calls, and the rough treatment continued. The last straw was when he and other entities woke me up again, in the middle of the night, to discuss chakras. Now there were others and that was enough for me! I came to the realization that these events had all the markings of a possession, and *nobody* possesses me!

The essence of the target was spiritually removed from the doll-baby by dissolving it in ammonia to soften the clay housing and removing the stone. Then both stones went into a bowl of ammonia. The entity's essence left both stones but instead used me as a replacement for his housing. After some convincing, he transferred back into the stones. Now the only other recourse that I could think of was to return the stones from whence they came, because any attempted binding rituals would be taking a huge risk against something so powerful.

So back to Chichen Itza I went, with the careless pilots from Cancún scaring me to death with their reckless handling of the plane—as if possession weren't punishment enough! Then, it was back to climbing up the steep pyramid, replacing the stones, and, once again, seeking the help of several people in order to return to the ground. Of course, don't forget I had to return to Cancún with the same crazy pilots. The trip back to the pyramid was not only expensive, but harrowing; however, my fear of that entity gave me the strength to confront my phobias.

The Aftermath: God Bless the Wiccans!

After performing aggressive self-cleansings, then cleansings of my home and my husband, I felt like a new woman. My cleansings allowed me to sleep and to resume functioning as a human being never to be bothered by that spiritual entity again. . . . However, a nagging feeling remained that something was trying to drag me down. Maybe it was just my body recuperating from the physiological ordeal caused by that entity?

On a business trip to Nevada, though, these nagging feelings returned and intensified. That's when I feared that my ties with that entity had not been completely severed. Without access to any of my own spiritual supplies, I consulted a friend who provided me with a phone number and address of a nearby Wiccan witch. Feeling frazzled, I just showed up at her door without calling first and interrupted an imminent coven meeting. I desperately pled my case. She welcomed me, a complete stranger, into her home and introduced me to all those present.

After all the witches there gave me a complete spiritual examination, they informed me that residual energy cords were attached to my aura. For hours, they lovingly and painstakingly detached them. From that day forward, I was completely free of that entity.

When detachment was completed, they refused payment. Each and every one of them instead requested a hug. Imagine these kind women inviting me into their home and terminating a coven meeting because this stranger's condition was more important! It was an eye-opener to the kindness of Wiccans and their knowledge of the spiritual realm. I am forever grateful to them and to all Wiccans.

Incidentally, the pyramid was eventually roped off due to mysterious mishaps and the local plane service was discontinued because of several accidents!

The Lessons Learned

Making mistakes is part of life. Correcting our mistakes and conquering self-revitalization give us wisdom. Therefore, welcome your mistakes because they are learning experiences, as well teaching opportunities. The following list contains the mistakes and life lessons I learned from my Chichen Itza adventure, which are now applied to all areas of life:

* **Ask questions and do your research.** My witch friend had advised me that the pyramid contained "power stones" but did not provide a clear definition. I did not ask questions nor did I research the pyramid, but instead just made assumptions. Years later, I learned that there had been hundreds of accounts of horrific events imposed on people, including archeologists, for taking from that pyramid.

* **If it seems too good to be true, then it is.** Although this is self-explanatory, it does provide

food for thought. If I had only stopped to think, I would have seen that if these stones were indeed "all-powerful," millions would have already been utilizing them for centuries. Additionally, they would have been quite costly!

* **Greed can be blinding.** This is a weakness defined as a selfish and excessive desire and widely considered immoral. The spiritual entity had obviously foreseen my greed.

* **Don't ignore bad feelings.** Always trust your gut feelings and first impressions. It's usually a communication from your Spirit Guides and/or Guardian Angels. Never ignore them by dismissing them as being merely judgmental or override feelings with rationalizations.

* **Don't dismiss someone else's negative feelings either.** The entity had no gripes against my friend Dru and instead chose to warn her. My response should have been to carefully consider her gut feelings about the stone and take them under advisement. Instead, my pretentious belief that I was the all-knowing psychic prevented me from listening to her. Now I have learned to listen to everybody, no matter who they are. It is imperative for a well-rounded knowledge base.

* **Never take what is not rightfully yours.** Basically, by taking those stones, I was stealing. Those stones belonged to the country of Mexico and, most likely, to that entity who guards and resides in that pyramid. Looking back on the event, I realize that entity had every right to be angry with me!

* **Look out for unhealthy attachments.** Not being able to part with the stone was a warning that it

was a psychologically unhealthy attachment. I should have been in control of that stone. Instead, the stone was in control of me.

* **Don't be seduced by individual results.** I was initially seduced by the stone's ability to control my target through the doll-baby. Unfortunately, they were isolated incidents and akin to a successful sales promotion that I bought into. After that, the stone had no further value to me, but I refused to see that because I was . . .

* **Falling in love with potential.** I held on to the stone believing that, one day, it would give me my desires. Obviously, that never happened, and instead, it began to ruin my life. But my false beliefs gave me the perseverance to continue my interactions with it.

In retrospect, I believe that the entity was not evil. Instead, he was merely punishing me for the theft. However, he behaved in a manner consistent with demonic possession, which we'll discuss later in the book.

For now, please keep in mind the lessons learned because they pertain to all areas of life and not just to attachments and the possession of objects.

Spiritual Entities within Objects

In the religion of Santería, as with many African Traditional Religions (ATRs), an essence of a sacred spiritual entity, rather than the entire entity itself, is summoned into a stone. If the entity agrees, an essence of its being enters the stone, which then serves as its housing. The stones are later placed in beautiful tureens and nurtured by the owner. In my story of Chichen Itza, it was not the entire spiritual entity within the stones I had, but rather his essence. This is why he was able to be within three stones at the same time while maintaining his guardianship of the temple atop the pyramid.

Essences are not necessarily housed in stones. They can be kept in different types of containers, and in some African tribes, they are even summoned directly into masks for ceremonial purposes. This is why people who have shopped in Africa and other parts of the world—or even just antique shops—have inadvertently purchased a ceremonial mask from which the essence has not been removed. Usually such masks have been stolen from the original owners. Nevertheless, the masks are possessed and a haunting is possible if the entity is unhappy.

The essence of a living being can also be stored in a container. The most common containers are effigies known as doll-babies, poppets, voodoo dolls, etc., although spellcasters can use other containers such as candles or jars. We simply take a piece of something called a "personal concern," which is anything containing DNA (deoxyribonucleic acid), to represent the essence of that being. As you may know, DNA is a blueprint that identifies each individual living being. Then, we call their name into the container to establish a sympathetic connection with someone at a distance. An essence of that being's spirit is now entrapped within the container.

Objects can house entire spirits as well. Although many different objects have been designed to house them—such as masks and stones—spirits can choose anything they please because the size of the housing does not matter.

Entities favor dolls, as representative of the people they are, when entering an object of their own accord. Additionally, children and numerous adults may name, animate, and bestow them personalities as a form of play. However, if a spiritual entity has entered a doll, these animating activities nurture the entities and, ultimately, give them strength. Thus, countless paranormal activities within a household stem from dolls.

John Zaffis is one of the world's foremost experts on haunted objects. I had the honor and privilege of meeting and learning from this great man about six years ago at a ghost hunt in Detroit, Michigan. In his book *Haunted by the Things You Love,* which provides in-depth descriptions of attached objects, he says that when spirits attach themselves to objects, they can initially be dormant for a long time. But when they wake up, the paranormal activities begin. I believe that the strength given to objects by animating and nurturing them will expedite the awakening.

A client of mine once had an original painting with the imagery of people on her bathroom wall. She said the painting was so beautiful that she "needed" to talk to the people in the image every day. Gradually, their faces started to change on a daily basis, as evidenced by the tons of photographs she would send me every day, until ultimately the images faded in and out and the body forms of humans changed to four-legged animals.

The painting was obviously possessed. Although it is inadvisable to engage in conversations with attached objects, the client feared that she would be punished by whatever had possessed the painting, so she told it that it was going to a loving home. Then, she mailed it to me for ritual disposal.

Spirits can also be ritually summoned into an object. This is performed for many reasons, but the most common ones are to bind a devious entity in order to prevent it from further malicious activities or to bind either a malicious or benevolent entity for self-serving purposes.

Entrapment of an entity out of self-interest is a common practice. We have all heard the tales about genies in bottles or lamps. In the fairy tales that are taught to us as children things are just lovely. We learn that they live in beautiful containers with all their needs and desires realized. Then the owner simply rubs the lamp, and the gorgeous genie who has unconditional love for the owner of the lamp appears, performs the will of the "master," then eagerly returns to its bottle. But the hard-core truth is that entities will be summoned and then ritually bound to a housing container, which acts as a jail. They are only released when forced to perform the bidding of the owner. Upon returning to their "master," they are forced back into their jail. These are enslaved entities that have no way of escape because the binding rituals have determined their fate.

Whether an object is possessed voluntarily or involuntarily in the end is not for you to ascertain or diagnose. It is just up to you to recognize the warning signs of an unwanted visitor in your presence or ownership:

* **An unnatural attraction to an object:** You can't stay away from the object or can't stop looking at it.

* **Uncomfortable or overly comfortable feelings:** If the object makes you feel uncomfortable, obviously that's a bad sign. However, the entity may attempt to entice you to keep it by emitting more than average feelings of comfort.

* **Hearing strange noises:** Do not dismiss any new noises.

* **Bad luck or bad experiences:** A sudden run of bad luck or distasteful experiences after taking an object into your possession and/or bringing it into your home is the entity emitting negativity.

* **Unfavorable changes in the personalities of one or more people in the household:** The energies of the entity within the object are affecting people.

* **Nightmares:** The entity within the object is again emitting negativity and could also be attempting a haunting.

* **Changes from negative to neutral emotions or feelings once it is away from you:** Take the suspicious object outside and leave it there. Once away from the object, if feelings of neutrality or positive vibrations come back, then, it is definitely the object causing the turmoil.

* **Seeing an unusual aura around the object:** Most objects do indeed have faint auras that are usually smoky white in color. However, if an object has an unusually radiant one, it is most likely the aura of the entity within the object. Also note that its aura may contain colors other than white.

* **Paranormal activity within the home:** The most common type of activities are moving, falling, or thrown objects; electrical mishaps; more than one appliance going awry in a short period of time; intrusive interference with telephone communications; and the flickering of lights.

* **Pets acting suspicious, aggressive, or fearful:** Pay attention to your pets' behaviors as their senses are more attuned to spiritual activities. If your pet is either continuously drawn to an object, unusually curious about it, or aggressive toward it, there is something within that object that is causing these behaviors. Obviously, if the pet is fearful of it, remove it from the house immediately.

Actions to Take If You Have a Possessed Object

Always bear in mind that you are in control. Yes, it is intimidating to have something from the supernatural realm invading your domain, but you must not show fear. Unless there are intense paranormal activities, you can handle it! Remember, if you are recognizing the possessed object early on, the entity has probably only recently emerged from a dormant state. In other words, it is like just awakening from a long sleep; therefore, it's a lot weaker than you are. So, gather your self-confidence, determination, strength of will, and faith because you will prevail. Just avoid these common mistakes:

* ⋆ Do not engage in any conversations with it.

* ⋆ Avoid any physical contact with it until you are ready to remove it.

* ⋆ While within the same dwelling, do not verbally state or reveal your plans to remove it—make it a surprise attack.

For the removal of the object, first spray it with Holy Water or water mixed with sea salt before you touch it. If it is a smaller object, it can be wrapped in whatever you have that has no value, such as plastic wrap or an old piece of cloth. If it is a larger object, wear gloves while handling it.

Attempt to return it to its original source or place of purchase. If this is not possible, it can be buried, preferably in a cemetery. If the object is small, a river will take it away.

If the object is too large, or if there are extreme paranormal activities associated with it, then contact a paranormal team or an expert in possessed objects.

Once the object is gone, perform a spiritual cleansing on yourself and a thorough spiritual cleansing of your home to remove any possible residual contamination.

Bewitched Objects

There are numerous ways to cast a spell on an object, which, in the language of Hoodoo, is also called "tricking an object." Although bewitched objects can be employed for love spells and other forms of magic, the harshest spells are those for cursing and crossing—the harmful intentions.

The object may contain herbs, roots, minerals, animal curios (sometimes, even entire dead animals are employed), and other ingredients intended for cursing. They can be gathered either as they are or in the form of powders, oils, or diluted bath crystals. Then, they are placed on and/or inside an object. The object used as the conduit can be anything from a toy to jewelry, stones, clothing, etc. However, the most common objects employed are dolls and stuffed animals.

The spellcaster then calls upon the spirits of the plants, minerals, and/or animals and gives them specific instructions on what to do. They will then make a sympathetic connection between the intended victim and the curse by visualizing the target and how the curse will take effect.

The object is then deployed to do its work. The bewitched object can be sent by mail, placed on or buried in the target's path, or even put within the target's home or in their clothing. Once the object is nearby, handled, or stepped upon by the target, the curse is activated.

Another way to curse an object is to make the sympathetic connection with the target and the curse by reciting magical incantations over the object while forcing cruel intentions into it.

Whatever method is utilized, these objects contain a vast amount of negative energies that can damage our auras. They do so by suppressing, attaching themselves to, or even penetrating our auras.

For more information about curses, see my book *Cursing and Crossing: Hoodoo Spells to Torment, Jinx, and Take Revenge on Your Enemies* (Lucky Mojo, 2017).

Recognizing and Discarding a Bewitched Object

Although many believe that a bewitched object will only affect the intended target, I tend to disagree. In my practice, many of my clients have interacted with tricked items that were not intended for them and yet were nonetheless negatively affected.

I once buried a cursed object on the property of a horrible neighbor with a clear and concise stated intention to bestow physical harm on this specifically named target. Unfortunately, someone else walked on that property and over the buried object only to fall and break his arm. Later that week, a worker fixing the sprinkler system on the target's property spent quite a long time standing directly over the buried object, and he was later struck by an automobile. (Thankfully, he survived.) Needless to say, I removed the item before the curse produced another innocent casualty.

Therefore, whether a bewitched object is intended for you or if you have inadvertently gained ownership, you need to know the warning signs and then get rid of it! The warning signs are about the same as those of a possessed object with the exception that the negative energies do not lie temporarily dormant. Instead, there will be an immediate feeling of discomfort followed by minor or major misfortunes with your health, social life, finances, personal relationships, business relationships, and/or emotional stability. Additionally, you will not have an attraction to the object. Paranormal activity may occur, but it is not commonplace.

Here is an easy way to discard a bewitched object:

* Always wear gloves when handling it.

* Soak it in a container of undiluted ammonia to deactivate the spell.

* Discard the first set of gloves.

* Don a different pair of gloves, remove the item from the ammonia, and throw it in an outside garbage can.

* Spiritually cleanse yourself and your home.

4

Negative People: The Suppressors and Deceivers

In this chapter, we will explore those types of people who exploit others through financial, sexual, emotional, and/or physical means in order to achieve their own success, higher social standing, or immediate gratification. These people are predators and accomplish their goals by implementing an array of tactics, including but not limited to winning our trust through deception, preying on our fears, providing false hopes and promises, the insinuations or actual threat of harm, and/or acts of physical violence.

These predators are successful because they have had years of trial and error experiences enabling them to become masters of their art. They have expertly learned the psychological makeup of people and are readily able to recognize our attributes as well as our vulnerabilities. Therefore, these predators know what they can take from us and how to do so, based on our weaknesses.

Although we will discuss the dynamics in greater detail, here are brief definitions of the most common types of predators:

* **The narcissist:** A person with an inflated sense of self and their own self-worth.

* **The sociopath:** An amoral and conscienceless person who seeks immediate gratification without feelings of remorse, guilt, or shame. Prone toward physical violence.

* **The thieves:** Those who steal what their victims have worked so hard to establish or acquire including money, material possessions, knowledge, and social/personal/business status or trick the victim into ongoing labor.

* **Liars, con artists, scammers:** Those who employ verbal and physical tricks to gain a victim's trust so that they can gain sexual favors or take money or gifts under false pretenses.

Collectively, all these various types can be thought of as suppressors and deceivers.

We Learn from Our Mistakes

Once a target has been identified, they will be turned into a victim through psychological manipulation. Beyond any loss of time, money, or status, the ultimate outcomes for the victim could be a loss of self-worth, self-esteem, and/or self-confidence. The victim can also suffer from a tremendous amount of anger, shame, guilt, or loss of self-respect. All of these unfavorable outcomes are both psychologically as well as spiritually unhealthy. The emotional and spiritual suppression could also lead to physiological illnesses.

Most of us, at some time or another, have fallen victim to at least one type of predator. But whether you are actively or have been retroactively involved in such a relationship, it is nonetheless a learning experience.

Yes, anger is normal for human beings when they face injustices. However, self-punishment does not serve any purpose here other than to continue giving the predator power over you even in their absence. We all strive for spiritual growth, but this cannot happen if we allow these unfavorable experiences to consume us.

Personally, I welcome these interactions with injustices because the experiences make me wiser and therefore better able to teach and guide those newly exposed to such encounters. Recently, I saw a meme on social media that rang true. It said that we learn from our elders not through what they know is right but rather because they have so much experience at being wrong! In other words, our elders have gained their wisdom the hard way: through actual interactions and mistakes. And as we all know, experience is the greatest teacher . . .

The Suppressors

Cruel predators show up in various settings determined to succeed without care for others. In numerous situations, they implement psychological tactics to make us doubt or question our own self-worth. I call these people "suppressors" because, if the predator succeeds, the victim is left with lingering psychological trauma that suppresses their aura, which sets up vulnerability to further attacks of the same or a different nature.

Bullying is deliberate and repeated attacks in an attempt to cause harm to those viewed as weaker. Bullies are usually the product of environmental factors such as strained relationships and poor social skills. However, the most severe types of suppressors are those who have a psychological disorder of a dissociative nature.

Narcissistic Personality Disorder

The Mayo Clinic states that the DSM-5 criteria for narcissistic personality disorder include the following features (but the individual does not need to meet all criteria):

- ★ Expecting to be recognized as superior even without achievements that warrant it.
- ★ Exaggerating achievements and talents.
- ★ Being preoccupied with fantasies about success, power, brilliance, beauty, or the perfect mate.
- ★ Believing that they are superior and can only be understood by or associate with equally special people.
- ★ Requiring constant admiration.
- ★ Having a sense of entitlement.
- ★ Expecting special favors and unquestioning compliance with their expectations.
- ★ Taking advantage of others to get what they want.
- ★ Having an inability or unwillingness to recognize the needs and feelings of others.
- ★ Being envious of others and believing others envy them.
- ★ Behaving in an arrogant or haughty manner.
- ★ Having an exaggerated sense of self-importance.

Narcissistic personality disorder crosses the border of healthy confidence into thinking so highly of yourself that you put yourself on a pedestal and value yourself more than you value all others. These individuals can fool others by making them think that they are simply confident people.

Sociopathic Personality Disorder

While the narcissist is focused on solely themselves and much more blatant in problem behaviors, sociopaths can be a lot more deceptive and somewhat sinister. According to HealthGuidance.org: "Sociopaths of course vary in their symptoms and might act differently in different cases. However, their main trait is presenting themselves as having the same empathy feelings and emotions as others when in fact they lack this emotional capacity. They are thus cold and manipulative and rarely see any problem with their actions."

What's the Difference Between a Sociopath and a Psychopath?

Many use the terms *sociopath* and *psychopath* interchangeably, but there is a difference. In a MedCircle YouTube interview entitled "Narcissist, Psychopath, or Sociopath: How to Spot the Difference," Ramani Durvasula, PhD, a renowned psychologist and author, says that a psychopath is born that way and has a different autonomic nervous system, whereas a sociopath is made, meaning it is learned behavior.

Whether a sociopath or psychopath, the behaviors are virtually identical. Here are a few of their traits according to HealthCare.org. Not all the criteria need to be met:

* Lack of empathy
* Cold, calculating nature
* Shallow emotions
* Narcissism
* Grandiose self-image

* Charming

* High IQ

* *Manipulative*

* Secretive

* Sexually deviant

* Sensitive to criticism

* Despotic/authoritarian

* Low tolerance for boredom

* Impulsive behavior

* Compulsive lying

* Most often involved in domestic violence cases

By examining the traits of these cunning people, it is easy to understand how they could manipulate others with their charming ways and get ahead with their lies and cheating. Many times, they will even attempt to steal your identity by claiming your work as their own. They will take what is yours and do whatever is necessary to achieve their goals.

They do not care about any consequences to others. Nor do they care about any physical pain, emotional pain and trauma, devastation, shock, distress, or grief that they have imposed. If they bankrupt you or your children, they don't care. Sadly, some scientific research speculates that one out of every twenty-four people is a sociopath.

Understanding the Behaviors of Suppressors

Hopefully, you have noticed the similarities in the characteristics of a narcissist and a sociopath. But it is essential that we familiarize ourselves with the behaviors of both, because their actions must be recognized and handled appropriately. There are millions of people who have fallen prey to their antics, and the results have been unadulterated negative consequences for these innocent victims.

Also keep in mind that narcissists and sociopaths are almost always the main players who fall under the categories of thieves (deceivers), liars, con artists, and scammers (enslavers). Remember, suppressors have a sense of entitlement.

If you are involved in a romantic relationship with a suppressor and now believe that your sense of self-worth has been diminished, it's time to walk away. Usually, they will make their partner believe that they are lucky to have that suppressor in their life because nobody else would want them. Well, the truth is always the exact opposite, and this brainwashing is a form of emotional abuse.

If, however, you are involved with a suppressor and believe there's no way out, there is. We'll get into emotional and physical abuse under the section on "Enslavement by the Need for Love and Belonging," but for now, please be aware that there are highly trained experts, knowledgeable in the psychological makeup of suppressors as well as the psychological devastations they impose on their victims. They know exactly how to help you, and you can contact them day or night. The National Domestic Violence Hotline contact number is available on their website TheHotline.org. Even if you are only suspicious of questionable behaviors, call the hotline and get the information you need. Don't be ashamed: knowledge is power.

If you are interacting with these people in other milieus, such as a workplace, be aware of their tactics. Document what they say and their actions. Keep a log but don't tell anyone what you are doing until you are ready to present your case to your superiors. Remember, most of these people haven't earned what they have taken and therefore do not have the knowledge or the experience to do what they claim for themselves. So it is inevitable that mistakes will be made. It never fails!

Protect yourself magically. It doesn't hurt to perform a Mirror Box Spell to assure that everything they do will bounce back to them.

A Mirror Box Spell: Frozen in Their Own Wrongdoing

Find a picture of the target with their eyes looking directly at the camera. Dab water on your fingertips and make the sign of the cross over the photo while saying "I baptize you in the name of the Father, the Son, and the Holy Spirit, and I name you (target's name)" or baptize or otherwise bless the picture according to your own faith. Put the picture aside and make your mirror box.

You will need six small mirrors and duct tape. Most craft stores sell the two-inch mirrors in a very inexpensive four-pack. However, if the two-inch mirrors are unavailable, four-inch mirrors will also work just as well. With two strips of duct tape, sticky side up, make a cross on a flat surface to form the foundation. Lay one mirror, shiny side up, in the middle of the cross of the tape. From there lay one mirror, shiny side up, at each side of the first mirror. Bring each mirror up, along with the duct tape, to form the five sides of a cube, with all the reflective sides of the mirrors facing the inside of the box.

Take the picture and firmly hold it in your hands and stare into the target's eyes. Firmly command the photo of the target: "Whatever you are and do will bounce back to you."

Place the picture inside the box. Now, complete the box with the last mirror facing inward to make a six-sided box. Seal the last mirror in place with duct tape. Then, rewrap the entire box with as much duct tape as possible to ensure that there are no cracks exposed between the mirrors.

Place the mirror box in the back of your freezer, leave it there, and forget about it!

An Emergency Mirror Spell

If you must wait for the six mirrors, take a picture of your target. Name and baptize it according to the previous instructions and state your command. Then, tape the image to the reflective side of any mirror.

The Deceivers

This category of harmful people encompasses those who steal not only material possessions, such as the common thief or burglar, but also those who rob us of the very essence of what we have worked so hard to achieve. Through deception, they will steal our business, our romantic partners, and/or our personal, professional, or social status. Once they have attained what they have set out to take, the victim is then disregarded as if they do not exist nor had ever existed.

In addition, many are capable of deceiving trusting people into assisting them by manipulating or tricking victims into ongoing hard work; financial, emotional, and/or public support; or knowledge contributions. The deceivers accomplish these feats by providing false hopes and dreams of immediate or future advances, but in reality, they either deliver a nightmare or nothing at all. Although these tactics can be implemented by virtually anyone, domestic violence abusers, power-mongers, and cult leaders are the ones who leverage them best.

Theft and Robbery

According to the National Center for Victims of Crime: "*Robbery* is when someone takes something you own from you by force or by threatening you. *Theft* is when someone takes something away from you without you knowing it . . ."

The definition of material theft and robbery also fits those who have stolen anything less tangible that we have acquired through hard work, such as our knowledge, business or romantic partners, or social/personal or business status. The ramifications, listed by the National Center for Victims of Crime, are also identical: "You might feel . . .

* Shocked, confused, angry, sad, powerless, or embarrassed.

* Very upset, even if what was taken wasn't worth a lot of money.

* Hopeless about whether anything can be done to get your property back.

* Suspicious of everyone around you."

These emotional consequences are quite overwhelming. But there are harsher ramifications beyond the loss of material possessions when a deceiver has taken what a target has slaved to attain. The victims find themselves in a position of subordination, while the deceivers gain the advantage over them. They did nothing to deserve what they have been awarded other than lying, cheating, and stealing to attain their goals while leaving the victims devastated. This is theft at its finest, and if the victim was strong-armed through intimidation or other coercive tactics, then it is robbery.

Alongside the emotions listed by the National Center for Victims of Crime, there's often an overwhelming feeling of betrayal. The most heartbreaking aspect associated with these situations may be the lack of understanding from peers or those the victims have thought of as friends. In many situations, these peers and pseudo-friends will show apathy toward the victim or even choose affection and friendship with the deceiver.

In these situations the victim can feel as though their life force has been drained or extracted from the very core of their souls. The victim's aura will have obviously been severely suppressed, allowing negative energies to cling to it.

The victim will need a spiritual cleansing bath to rid the aura of negativities, followed by healing spells for aura replenishment. Later, empowerment techniques can restore strength and courage. Once the aura has regained strength, then spells to bind the deceiver from further harm and freeze them out of the life of the victim are most certainly warranted!

Spiritual Cleansing Baths

Spiritual cleansing baths are intended to clear the aura of negative energies that have adhered to it. These baths are not meant to remove the daily physical dirt that our bodies naturally accumulate. Therefore, if necessary, a regular bath or shower designed to remove physical dirt or grime from the body ought to be performed at least a few hours prior to any spiritual bath.

Precautions

Please keep in mind that if you have open sores or wounds on your skin, including rashes, avoid any baths until you have first consulted with a physician. The same applies to allergies. Although the more aggressive bathing rituals will be presented later in this book, ensure that you have no allergies to any of the bath ingredients before you engage in a full bath with these ingredients.

Bath 1: Holy Water Bath

Fill a bathtub with warm water.

Add four ounces of Holy Water to the bathtub water and agitate the water to disperse.

Bath 2: Ammonia Bath

Fill a bathtub with warm water.

Add only one tablespoon of ammonia to the bathtub water and agitate the water to disperse.

Remember, the adage "More is better" does *not* apply to ammonia. Do *not* increase the amount of ammonia as it is a skin irritant.

Bath 3: Sea Salt Bath

Fill a bathtub with warm water.

Add one-quarter cup of sea salt to the bathtub water and agitate the water to evenly disperse the salt.

Bathing Instructions

Remove clothing and enter the bathtub nude. Immerse yourself, head included, a total of thirteen times while reciting Psalms 23 (see chapter 1), the Lord's Prayer, or both. Prior to closing your last recitation with the word *Amen*, state your plea to remove all negative energies from your aura. If you are wearing hair extensions or weaves, only immerse yourself up to your neck. Attempt to remain in the bathtub for thirteen minutes.

Once you are ready to leave the bathtub, do not rinse yourself off with water. Instead, walk out of the bathtub and lightly blot yourself dry preferably with a white towel. Put on your clothes. Remove the bathtub stopper and as the water drains, state aloud that all negative energies are to leave immediately. Anoint the back of your neck and head with Protection Oil, Blessing Oil, or Holy Oil for protection. If oils are not available, spray Holy Water to these areas.

It is highly recommended to perform the bathing ritual for thirteen consecutive days. Wait for at least twenty hours after a spiritual bath to take a regular bath or shower designed to remove physical dirt or grime from the body.

THE LORD'S PRAYER

Our Father, Who art in heaven

Hallowed be Thy Name; Thy kingdom come.

Thy will be done on earth as it is in heaven.

Give us this day our daily bread,

and forgive us our trespasses, as we forgive those who trespass against us;

And lead us not into temptation but deliver us from evil.

For the kingdom, and the power, and the glory are yours now and forever. AMEN.

Healing Spell

Healing is the process of restoring health to an unbalanced, injured, or diseased organism and to make that organism sound or whole again. Once the aura has been cleansed of the spiritual dirt that has suppressed or damaged it, a healing spell will assist in restoring the aura to that state of wholeness.

A simple healing spell is to obtain a blue nine-inch jumbo candle and inscribe the words "Heal from Hurt" nine times on the candle. Do this in a spiral from the bottom to the top of the candle. Anoint the candle with Healing Oil, then roll it in Healing Incense.

If Healing Oil and Healing Incense are unavailable, crush one or more of the healing herbs listed below. Anoint your candle with olive oil, then roll it in the crushed herbs.

* **Althaea leaves** (*Althaea officinalis*): Used for medical and spiritual healing.

* **Angelica root powder** (*Angelica archangelica*): A powerful healer.

* **Boneset leaves** (*Eupatorium ageratoides*): Rids energies that have affected one's health.

* **Caraway** (*Carum carvi*): Heals and protects.

* **Self-heal, all-heal, woundwort** (*Prunella vulgaris*): A healing herb.

Obtain a picture of yourself with your eyes showing. Write your birth name and birth date on the photo—but not across the eyes. Place the picture in a fireproof candleholder with the image of facing upward. Place the candle directly over your picture. Light the candle and recite aloud Psalm 41, which is about people who have caused harm to another or when healing is needed. Prior to closing the recitation with the word *Amen*, tell God exactly what has happened and ask God to heal you.

PSALM 41

1 Blessed is he that considereth the poor: the LORD will deliver him in time of trouble.

2 The LORD will preserve him, and keep him alive; and he shall be blessed upon the earth: and thou wilt not deliver him unto the will of his enemies.

3 The LORD will strengthen him upon the bed of languishing: thou wilt make all his bed in his sickness.

4 I said, LORD, be merciful unto me: heal my soul; for I have sinned against thee.

5 Mine enemies speak evil of me, When shall he die, and his name perish?

6 And if he come to see me, he speaketh vanity: his heart gathereth iniquity to itself; when he goeth abroad, he telleth it.

7 All that hate me whisper together against me: against me do they devise my hurt.

8 An evil disease, say they, cleaveth fast unto him: and now that he lieth he shall rise up no more.

9 Yea, mine own familiar friend, in whom I trusted, which did eat of my bread, hath lifted up his heel against me.

10 But thou, O LORD, be merciful unto me, and raise me up, that I may requite them.

11 By this I know that thou favourest me, because mine enemy doth not triumph over me.

12 And as for me, thou upholdest me in mine integrity, and settest me before thy face for ever.

13 Blessed be the LORD God of Israel from everlasting, and to everlasting. Amen, and Amen.

Nine-inch candles take about twenty-eight hours without interruption to burn. Attempt to allow the candle to burn completely without snuffing it out. Sometimes, people will set it in a porcelain sink, bathtub, or shower to allow the candle to completely burn.

Once the candle has been fully consumed, take the candle wax remains with the picture and either bury it all in your backyard or wrap it in a white cloth and place it under your bed.

Rebuilding Self-Esteem and Empowerment

Mending one's self-esteem is easier said than done, especially after emotionally traumatic events that have changed or minimized self-perceptions. It takes effort to improve self-esteem but, with determination, progress will ultimately give you back a sense of empowerment.

Carrying one of the following roots and/or applying oils of the same name greatly help to improve power, mastery, self-esteem, and personal strength. The following roots have helped many of my clients to realize their desires:

* **John the Conqueror root** increases personal power and mastery.
* **Master root** increases self-esteem.
* **Solomon's seal root** assists in gaining respect and favor.

But always remember with any type of spiritual assistance that your behaviors must complement your magic while your magic must complement your behaviors. The practice of magic, the utilization of amulets, etc., only *enhances* your chances for success by acting as a backup to your own performance. Actively employing techniques to improve one's self-esteem is what is truly essential:

* **Do things that make you happy.** Take the time to treat yourself to activities that you enjoy.
* **Accept yourself for who you are.** Remember that nobody is—or ever will be—perfect.

* **Exercise.** When the body is happy and healthy, it releases "feel-good" hormones.

* **Take daily vitamins.** These improve overall health and thought processes.

* **Surround yourself with pleasant people and conversations.** While in the healing process avoid anyone or anything that causes you discomfort.

Binding the Suppressor or Deceiver

Take a wallet-size photo of the deceiver with their eyes showing, and write the target's birth name and birth date across the picture but do not write across the eyes.

With black yarn, wrap the picture while repetitiously saying aloud: "I bind (target's name) from doing harm to me and to others." Keep doing this until the picture is no longer visible.

Now, tie thirteen knots while repeating the same command. Although your spell ought to look like a small ball of yarn now, it doesn't matter, as long as the picture is completely covered.

Bury this in a cemetery or in the woods or throw it in a sewer or river to send the person away.

Freezing the Suppressor or Deceiver Out of Your Life

Spell 1

If you don't have a picture of the deceiver, write the target's birth name and birth date on both sides of a torn piece of brown paper bag with a pencil. Hold the name paper firmly in both hands while stating aloud that your target will be frozen from doing harm. Place the paper in a small container and add water. Cover the container with a black cloth, then secure the cloth by tying or taping it. Place this in the back of the freezer and forget that it is there.

Spell 2

Take a picture of the target and write their birth name and birth date across the picture but do not write across the eyes. Turn the picture to the left and cross the name with the command: "You are frozen from doing harm." Wrap this in a paper towel then place it over a piece of aluminum foil, shiny side up. Generously moisten the paper towel with water, wrap this with the foil, and place it in the back of the freezer.

Enslavement by the Need for Love and Belonging

When I was in nursing school, we learned about Abraham Maslow's now famous hierarchy of needs. He contended that all human beings strive to achieve self-actualization. However, in order to accomplish this, we must first sequentially satisfy more pressing needs.

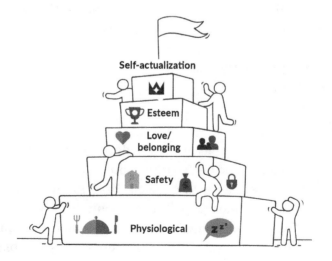

Maslow's model, represented by a pyramid, depicts each need that must be fulfilled before we can strive to attain the next level. At the very bottom of the pyramid, we must first satisfy our physiological needs, such as food, water, and health, followed by our needs for safety and shelter. Once these are fulfilled, we seek love and belonging, which includes acceptance by others and intimacy. If all the levels of the pyramid have been realized, we then strive to achieve our need for self-esteem and then finally self-actualization.

Unfortunately, when we are on the level of achieving love and belonging, we can sometimes get into trouble with the wrong people! Most deceivers and suppressors are clever sociopaths who easily recognize other people's needs and desires. They then manipulate these innocent folks into believing that they can help them to achieve their dreams—but only if the victim reciprocates and helps them too. Once the victim's trust has been gained, that person is instead tricked or forced into submissiveness—and sometimes even enslavement—in order to help the manipulator to achieve their own self-serving agendas.

You can often see this process in both intimate relationships and group structures.

Domestic Violence

According to the National Domestic Violence Hotline:

Domestic violence (also called intimate partner violence or IPV) includes behaviors that physically harm, arouse fear, prevent a partner from doing what they wish or force them to behave in ways they do not want. It includes the use of physical and sexual violence, threats and intimidation, emotional abuse and economic deprivation. Many of these different forms of domestic violence/abuse can be occurring at any one time within the same intimate relationship.

Sadly, once someone is enslaved with IPV, there are many reasons the victim remains in the dysfunctional relationship. These range from fear of retaliation to believing that abuse is normal. Financial insecurity, embarrassment, disabilities, cultural and/or religious beliefs, and language barriers all play their parts as well. Some victims even believe that their spirit is dead and there's no hope.

But, there is indeed hope! The National Domestic Violence Hotline has many options and resources. So, once again, as I cannot stress enough that if you are a victim of domestic violence, please contact TheHotline.org. And perform as many ritual protection techniques as possible. The tools provided to enhance your self-esteem will assist in generating the confidence to take action for escape and recovery.

Cohesive Group Dynamics

Groups form when there is a psychological bond between individuals or when people share the same social categories such as similar professions, the same interests or beliefs, being on teams, etc. Once a group is established, the individuals develop shared norms, roles, and attitudes, which the members internalize to define themselves and their behaviors. Structures including values and communication patterns, and status differentials like leadership roles also develop.

Group membership ought to provide its participants with emotional, instrumental, and/or informational support. Additionally, all group structures ought to give a sense of acceptance and, most importantly, a sense of belonging.

Dysfunctional Group Dynamics

Beware the warning signs of dysfunctional groups—for example, lack of accountability or blame-placing. One frequent dysfunction that can lead to victimization is unhealthy competition. Suppressors will elevate themselves to undeserved prestigious positions while dragging down or demoting the hardworking, knowledgeable members in order to keep them at bay. The group may even exploit a victim's knowledge or status for their personal gain. Most obvious to the victim is the lack of recognition and a sense of belonging.

Sometimes the signs are blatant, but other times, they will be subtle. First and foremost, trust your gut instincts, and then pay attention to the actions of the group. When words and actions don't align, do not believe the words. After all, victims may hear that they are wanted, but that is only because the victims' contributions are needed in order to advance selected group members.

If a group you are involved with is draining or stealing victims' energies without any positive reciprocation, perform spiritual cleansing baths and aura-strengthening techniques to replenish any weakening of your aura. Realize there are other cohesive groups deserving and appreciative of your valuable contributions and seek those out instead. (Just be prudent to avoid jumping from the frying pan into the fire!) Walk away, with pride, from the dysfunction.

Liars, Con Artists, and Scammers

There are various reasons that humans lie. In innocent circumstances there may be no intent to deceive, but instead the person lying may believe that the truth could be hurtful to the other person and does so with the intent to protect them. Sociopathic lying, on the other hand, is of a different nature. It is the technique or "art" of creating elaborate lies, deceptions, and schemes for their own personal gain without regard for what the consequences might be for the victim. In other words, they tell lies without conscience.

Sociopathic liars are involved in confidence tricks—i.e., cons and scams—in which they employ verbal and physical trickery to gain the trust of a mark. Once they have obtained that trust, the con artist will take money, materialistic belongings, or sexual favors from the victim under false pretenses.

Most frequently, the media relays stories of older people being tricked out of their life savings, younger people being tricked into prostitution, or romantic partners being tricked out of money and material possessions. We rarely hear or read about victims who have been scammed or conned by a pseudo-spiritual worker or psychic. Although these particular crimes are as old as time, with social media now connecting millions of people, psychic and spiritual scammers are on the rise.

Confidence tricks exploit human weaknesses such as greed, dishonesty, fear, vanity, lust, compassion, etc. But psychic or spiritual cons particularly exploit the naivety, desperation, fears, and tendency toward embarrassment of the victim.

Psychic and Spiritual Cons

There are excellent spiritual practitioners in our world, but sadly, there are just as many who are not. The con artist prepares the foundation by utilizing social media venues to advertise their level of excellence and power, as well as recruiting friends to deliver testimonials regarding the scammer's expertise.

Once the approach, or contact, has been made by the victim, the scammer performs what is referred to as "the build-up," where the victim is charmed by the con artist. Then the scammer convinces the victim that they are all-knowing, also known as "the convincer" stage, by utilizing cold, warm, and hot reading techniques:

* ★ **Cold readings:** Analyzing a person's ethnicity, level of education, language, age, manner of speech, body language, or other characteristics and then

employing high-probability guesses while keeping an eye out for feedback on these guesses.

* **Warm readings:** The scammer makes statements that refer to all human beings. Examples would include generalities like "Someone around you has died" or "Someone around you has dark eyes."

* **Hot readings:** This method utilizes foreknowledge. Among a vast array of techniques employed, the most widely used are internet searches, such as "People Search," to acquire a vast history, Google Earth, and checking the victim's social media.

Next comes the "hurrah stage" when the scammer exploits the naivety, desperation, and/or fears of the victim and convinces the person to give the scammer either big money for spellcasting or sexual favors. Usually, they convince the victim through insinuation or direct threats that they have the ability to curse the victim if they do not comply. Sometimes, by exploiting the victims' tendencies toward embarrassment, there are ongoing payments.

Cults

In extreme cases, some scammers may feel so empowered as to form their own group of followers. By implementing confidence tricks, the scammer may form the foundation of a cult under the guise of having supreme powers and insight.

In a CBS network interview entitled "How to Identify a Cult, Six Expert Tips," psychologist Steve Eichel, a recognized international cult expert, identifies several warning signs:[1]

* "Beware of any kind of pressure: any kind of pressure to make a quick decision about becoming

---

[1] CBS News. *How to Identify a Cult: Six Expert Tips.* CBSNews.com.

involved in any intensive kind of activity or organization."

★ "Be wary of any leader who proclaims him- or herself as having special powers or special insight . . ."

★ "The group is closed—there may be outside followers, but there's usually an inner circle that follows the leader without question and that maintains a tremendous amount of secrecy."

★ "The group uses deceptive means, typically, to recruit new members, and then will subject its members to an organized program of thought reform, or what most people refer to as brainwashing."

★ "Typically cults also exploit their members financially, psychologically, emotionally, and, all too often, sexually."

★ "A very important aspect of cult is the idea that if you leave it, horrible things will happen to you . . ."

Cults Are Not Always of a Religious Nature

These groups may be of any type and not necessarily religious, but they do share tendencies with the well-known religious cults. According to David Tormsen, in an article on ListVerse.com entitled "10 Insane Non-Religious Cults," these shared tendencies include:

★ Deceptive recruitment tactics

★ Unquestioning commitment to the leader

★ Punishment of dissent (in other words, being punished for disagreeing, having objections, or expressing dissatisfaction with the policies or practices)

I will share with you just one of my two personal experiences with cultlike groups.

About fifteen years ago, while living in Florida temporarily, I was pressured into joining a dog training group by
the close friends of a dog trainer. They insisted that this
trainer was the best in the business and knew everything
about German Shepherds dogs. They also assured me that
my dogs would win big trophies under his guidance.

When I met him, he seemed to be a calm, caring, and
charming man. Everybody in the group adored the leader,
yet it appeared that their dogs were not progressing as
far as they should have. Nevertheless, I joined the group,
believing that with my vast experience in this field, his
additional tutelage would take me to a national competition level. His fees were exorbitant, but my hopes of gran-
deur prevailed.

To the majority of us, the trainer instead provided
stagnancy while failing to deliver enough time or information for us to complete our goals. He did, however, show
favoritism toward his close friends by giving them extra
training time while attempting to promote them as his
training assistants. Because the favored ones neither had
the knowledge nor the experience to teach, the scenario
was comparable to first graders trying to educate college
graduates about the sport. Being bold and knowing that
my own knowledge of the sport had been downplayed, I
resisted these inept neophyte teachers, and that's when my
troubles started because the entire group began treating
me as an outcast.

Nevertheless, the trainer continued to charge us ridic-
ulously high fees on an ongoing basis by playing on our
dreams of great progress soon to be realized. While others
gladly gave him their money, it was more than apparent
to me that we were instead paying for false hopes, and
my displeasure was more than obvious. After "daring" to
amicably confront him about my dogs' lack of progress

in a specific area that required his alleged expertise, this calm man turned into a monster, screaming and blame-placing rather than admitting that he did not provide the paid-for services. After that, his behaviors toward me were condescending.

Weeks later, our group had a competitive event known as a trial. I did not enter my dogs in the trial, so my participation was solely as an observer. Sadly, every single person failed the trial, including the trainer's inner circle of friends.

Later, his inner circle pressured the entire group into expressing their gratitude to the trainer. They loyally succumbed, emphatically sharing their appreciation to the trainer. They suffered great financial losses and unadulterated failures, but instead were pressured into thanking him because they most likely feared punishment of dissent (the repercussions of opposition). They behaved as if they had been brainwashed.

I left the group that very day, never to return, because I realized the group had all the markings of a cult, including:

* There was pressure to join the group.
* They had deceitful recruitment tactics.
* The leader was considered an expert.
* The group had an inner circle.
* The group followed the leader without question.
* The group was exploited for money.
* There was punishment of dissent.

Aside from the fear that bad things will happen to members if they leave a cult, there appears to be one other strong sustaining factor, and that is false hope. Often members truly believe that there will be future rewards or successes if they remain obedient and loyal to their leaders. Unfortunately, the rewards and/or successes rarely happen, and the members are perpetually kept dreaming for their day to arrive.

How to Avoid Psychic and Spiritual Scams and Cons

Of the utmost importance is to trust your gut instinct and do not sideline it with rationalization or justification! So often, we want to see the good in others and wrongfully assume that we all share honorable values. Other times, we want to believe the con artist because they are charming or seem sincere. The bottom line? If something doesn't feel right, look right, or "rubs you the wrong way," then walk away! Other steps to take are:

* **Perform internet searches.** Check to see if there are any complaints against the worker. Enter their name followed by the words *scam, rip-off,* and/or *complaints,* and you may find results—but not in all cases if victims are fearful of retaliation.

* **Be wary of boundless credentials.** If the worker professes to be a master of a copious number of spiritual practices but their age is inconsistent with the years it takes to master each, then do the math! Also remember that a jack-of-all-trades is a master of none.

* **Do not get seduced with "free readings."** In most cases—but not all—this is the foundation work for soliciting money for spellwork or sexual favors.

* **Recognize the mechanics of cold, warm, and hot readings.** Be neutral when obtaining a reading and do not provide the worker with information to confirm or deny any open-ended statements.

* **Keep foremost in your mind if something seems too good to be true, then it is.** Spellwork is not

guaranteed to work, rather it is an attempt to facilitate your desires. Anyone who guarantees manifestation is a liar.

* **Know the lures sexual predators use.** Having intercourse with a godparent is forbidden in most spiritual practices, especially in the religions of Santería and Palo. Also, any practitioner using phrases such as "erotic séances" or "erotic hypnosis" should be treated with suspicion.

* ***Never* display or verbalize desperation.** Saying things like "I'll do anything" or "I will pay anything" for your desires only displays your willingness to become a mark.

* **Do not disclose your income or your profession.** Your income and your profession have nothing to do with the services you are seeking.

* **Steer clear of practitioners imposing personal beliefs.** Good spiritual workers will not impose their religious, political, or other personal beliefs on their clients. This is a service industry that caters to clients, not vice versa.

* **If you are pressured for an immediate initiation, walk away.** Telling clients that they need to be initiated immediately into a faith is most often a scam. Although immediate initiations do legitimately exist, those cases are usually related to health issues.

* **Do not pay for outrageous spells.** For example, a client once paid a scammer $70,000 to sacrifice a horse for her loved one to return. The lover never came back to her.

* **Know that spells do not have to be performed immediately.** This is a common con, where the

scammer promotes urgency by professing that a spells must be performed immediately or else there will be dire consequences. Unless there are health issues, spells can wait.

* **Don't repay.** If the spell didn't work the first time, don't pay for another.

* **Do comparative research of prices.** Once a spell-caster quotes a price for spellwork, check other spellcasters' prices to ensure industry standards are being followed.

* **Don't be conned by threats of a curse.** This is the most common and horrific scam of all. I have heard more than 600 complaints from fearful people who had been victimized by this confidence trick and have either lost thousands upon thousands of dollars or are making ongoing payments to the con artist for fear of being cursed. There is no curse! The con artist instills and uses fear to suppress the client's aura and authentic truth. That suppression is what makes them believe they are cursed. As I have told hundreds of clients, I wrote a book titled *Cursing and Crossing* and have *never* mentioned my abilities or knowledge about cursing, hexing, or jinxing because it is not my desire to instill feelings of fear, apprehension, or reservations toward me.

* **Remember the words of Nelson Mandela**. If you have been a victim, do *not* feel ashamed. Instead, follow the advice of this great man: "Do not judge me by my successes—judge me by how many times I fell down and got back up again."

If, however, the threat of a curse has caused you lingering fear, perform the St. Michael Protection Spell.

St. Michael Protection Spell

Obtain a red or white candle. With a pencil, inscribe the word *protection*, followed by your name, followed by the word *protection* again on it in a spiral from bottom to top. If your name is Jane Doe, the inscription would be: "protectionjanedoeprotection."

Then, anoint the candle with Holy Oil or Protection Oil. Place a picture of yourself, with eyes showing, facing up, in a candleholder, then position the candle over the picture. Place this in front of an image of St. Michael. Light the candle and recite this prayer aloud:

> *St. Michael the Archangel, defend us in battle, be our protection against the malice and snares of the Devil. May God rebuke him we humbly pray; and do thou, O Prince of the Heavenly host, by the power of God, thrust into hell Satan and all evil spirits who wander through the world for the ruin of souls.* **(State your particular petition.)** *Amen.*

5

Illness: The Effects on the Infirmed and on the Caregivers

The information and suggestions provided in this chapter do not in any way, shape, or form act as a replacement or substitution for professional medical care. Therefore, if you are suffering from a physical or emotional illness, please consult a licensed physician immediately! Now that that is out of the way, let's go into the spiritual aspects of illnesses for those suffering and those caring for them.

There is an intricate and interrelated balance between the three forces of mind, body, and spirit, as they directly sustain one another. If one of these forces is compromised, the other two will be affected. Physical illnesses can influence the mind, as well as our spiritual wellness, whereas an emotional illness can affect our physical and spiritual well-being. And, as we already know, spiritual suppression can impact us both emotionally and physically.

Furthermore, if illnesses are improperly managed, the consequences surrounding the infirmed can also vastly, and negatively, affect the caregiver's emotional, physical, and spiritual well-being. Thus, because knowledge facilitates empowerment, the purpose of this chapter is to familiarize both the infirmed and the caregivers, with the effects of illnesses and how to hopefully alleviate as many unfavorable conditions as possible. Additionally, we'll discuss measures to protect both from further harmful energies.

Illness is a period of unhealthy conditions affecting the body, mind, and spirit caused by the body or mind being harmed from an organ or part that is unable to work as it usually does. An illness can have an acute onset—a sudden arrival that is usually short-lived, or it can be of a chronic nature—defined as lasting for a long time, or it can be of a progressive nature—meaning that it is chronic with a continual worsening over time. When we face a shift from our normal functioning, we will also experience stress, defined as a physical, mental, or emotional factor resulting in bodily or mental tension. If unmanaged, the stress will exacerbate the health issue.

Clearly, an unmanaged illness produces a vicious cycle consisting of the initial health problem that will induce stress, which, in turn, worsens the health problem. Furthermore, these dynamics will lead to physical, emotional, and spiritual immunosuppression, leaving us susceptible to other illnesses, infections, diseases, and various additional negative events.

The physiological consequences induced by stress consist of problems such as headaches, fatigue, cardiovascular incidents, sleep deprivation, gastrointestinal problems, loss of libido, and musculoskeletal problems. When these surface, they can produce worry, frustration, anger, and/or fear, leading to mood changes.

According to the Mayo Clinic, such mood changes can include anxiety, restlessness, lack of motivation, lack of focus, feeling overwhelmed, irritability, sadness, and depression. These events, in turn, produce behavioral changes such as over- or undereating, angry outbursts, drug or alcohol abuse, or social withdrawal. These mood and behavioral changes then produce further physiological debilitation.

The aura receives all messages as the feedback loop spirals downward and is affected in the extreme. It is weakened and suppressed by all the negative impacts, which drain it of energy. These energy drains will produce further worry and frustration in addition to the mood and behavioral changes from the physical stress. If the energy drains are prolonged, they can lead to tears and holes in the auric field, which can make us susceptible to additional physical health problems.

As you can see, the mind, body, and spiritual shields are all interrelated and dependent on one another! However, there are other spiritual consequences to an aura with tears and/or holes as well. These cavities make us susceptible to other forces, and because negativity attracts more of the same, the turmoil caused by the physiological and/or emotional disorders can attract malevolent forces.

Know the Signs and Symptoms of Attracting Malevolent Forces

In an article by Health Day News for Healthier Living titled "Illness: The Mind-Body Connection," it is stated that: "When a person is depressed, the whole body suffers. Illness strikes more frequently, and the road to recovery grows more difficult. Likewise, people who enjoy emotional health are better able to fend off diseases and enjoy better health during a chronic illness."

Therefore, illnesses must be managed not just physically, but also emotionally and spiritually in order for the healing process to commence. But we must first recognize the signs and symptoms of the negativity we are combating in order to restore emotional health.

Remember Maslow's hierarchy of needs discussed in chapter 4? Our most basic need is that of survival. An illness can trap a person on that level, lacking any desire to fulfill other needs until the basic one has been satisfied. In other words, they are "stuck."

However, if the illness goes on too long without proper management and a victim succumbs to it, they may experience apathy, hopelessness, listlessness, lack of happiness, addictions, etc. Some people refer to these accumulated feelings as "soul loss," which may present as irritability, hostility, aggressive feelings or behaviors, and excessive suspiciousness.

Often they exhibit no interest in their appearance, and ultimately, there will be social withdrawal, isolation, and loneliness. This is a dangerous stage because loneliness deprives us of the sensory stimulation of sight, sound, touch, and hearing, and therefore opens an opportunity for a malevolent spiritual entity to deceptively satisfy these needs. In fact, the entity may even trick the victim into feelings of being loved as well as providing a false sense of importance. When this occurs, the entity may be granted what it yearns for: an invitation.

Improving Emotional Health and Combating Negative Forces

Keep in mind that not only does negativity attract negativity, but negative forces seek out situations and circumstances that provide an opportunity for them to enter and insert themselves in our lives. By avoiding what appeals to them and providing both an atmosphere and attitude that repulse them, the following techniques and positive stimulation will not only improve your overall health, but will also repel negativity:

* **Sunlight:** The sun has many benefits for us humans. First, exposure to sunlight stimulates and strengthens the aura. Second, scientists have discovered that the sun also stimulates and increases our natural levels of an antidepressant in our brains called serotonin. It is now believed that the lack of sunlight and the associated decrease in serotonin production are the cause of seasonal affective disorder (SAD). Most importantly, it is also believed that lower vibrations or negative forces cannot exist in the presence of the sun. Get exposure to direct sunlight by either opening a window or taking a daily brief walk outside on a sunny day.

* **Fresh air:** This has both a cleansing and calming effect on our brains. It also acts as a disinfectant that kills bacteria. Try to keep windows opened, preferably with a screen to shield out insects, as much as possible. However, do prevent exposure to cool drafts.

* **Bathing:** The skin is the largest organ of the body, and bathing—which soothes it—will send calming signals to the aura. Additionally, bathing improves our circulation as well as leaving us feeling refreshed and rejuvenated. The union of humans with water is also a spiritual encounter. No wonder people sing in the shower!

* **Music that appeals to the infirmed:** Music is a phenomenon that affects all human beings. (I see my animals favorably affected, too.) The thrill of music is due in part to its ability to manipulate

emotions by triggering memories or producing fantasies. Ensure that the music you listen to is appealing to the infirmed rather than just the caregiver. A musical piece may be aesthetically pleasing to one but repulsive to another.

* **Television:** Favorable programs not only provide positive stimuli for our senses of sight and sound, but they can help people to keep abreast of the news and current events, provide education, facilitate critical thinking about society and the world, and keep our minds occupied with other thoughts in order to divert attention away from the illness.

* **Pleasant odors:** Odors enter the nose and travel to nerve receptors, which take the smells to the brain for interpretation. Certain odors, such as the smell of lavender, will cause the brain to enhance sleep and alleviate stress, anxiety, and even some types of pain. Other odors may stimulate pleasant memories. Aromatherapy—which is a science utilizing aromatic essences from plants to create balance, harmony, and the promotion of the health of the body, mind, and spirit—has been very successful in lifting the spirits of the ill.

* **Color therapy:** It is believed that certain colors affect our moods. PsyWeb, a resource for depression and mental health, relays what has been identified by esoteric practitioners as the colors mostly used to treat depressive disorders:

  + **Orange** treats depression by increasing alertness and concentration and decreasing feelings of dread.

  + **Blue** reduces tension and helps with anxiety, depression, and sleep cycles.

- **Indigo** has a calming effect for anxiety.
- **Violet** relaxes the mind and body.

★ **Light therapy:** Mostly employed for seasonal affective disorder (SAD), a special white or sometime blue-tinted light is used to simulate the sun and changes the body's biochemistry.

★ **The power of touch:** Interpersonal touch is a basic aspect of most living creatures, and the need for touch is ingrained in our biology. It is one of our basic senses. Not only do we crave this type of stimulation, but it is usually the first sense that we encounter. When dogs are born, they cannot see or hear for the first ten days of their lives, and yet, they seek their mother for milk, cleansing, and warmth through their sense of touch. Newborn babies don't understand very much other than the touch of their caregivers as well. They hold and caress us, while providing food, warmth, comfort, and security. So living creatures are programmed to associate touch with ease and security. Touch is a nonverbal form of delivering comfort and can be shared, or reciprocated, in different ways such as receiving a massage, holding another's hand, rubbing an arm or shoulder, a hug, and the list goes on. Personally, I am a hugger! Although it is annoying to a few people, the majority respond with joy, and it becomes a mutual, beneficial, and therapeutic event.

★ **Grounding techniques for anxiety:** Grounding is a technique that helps us be more connected with the earth. There are numerous exercises to do this readily available on the internet, ranging from meditation to psychological therapeutic techniques—which are highly recommended. However, if you are pressed for time, a few quick methods can include walking barefoot, laying on the grass, and/or hugging a tree. All have shown to be beneficial. The mineral kyanite, one of the only two crystals that do not need cleansing—the other being citrine—because it does not retain energies, has numerous beneficial properties, including grounding. By holding this crystal in your hands for a couple of minutes, you should feel a sense of ease.

* **Laughter:** As we have all been told throughout our lives, laughter is the best medicine. Why is it medicinal? Because laughter provokes chemical responses in our bodies such as the release of endorphins, which act as natural painkillers in addition to it being a general "feel-good" chemical. In other words, it gives us a natural sense of euphoria and strengthens the aura. Of equal importance is the fact that negative forces are repulsed by laughter.

Most Importantly

In an article entitled "Coping with Chronic Illness and Depression" on WedMD, the following outstanding advice is provided:

* **Avoid isolation.** Reach out to family and friends or ask your health care provider about support groups.

* **Learn as much about your illness as possible.** Knowledge is power, and it will give you a sense of control over your condition.

* **Make sure you have medical support from experts.** Ensure that you can talk to them openly

regarding ongoing questions and concerns and
make certain that they are readily available.

* **Look into pain management.** Talk with your physician about pain management, as there's no reason
to endure pain.

* **Speak up if your medication is bringing you
down.** If your medication does not agree with you
and is interrupting your normal daily activities,
talk to your doctor about alternative treatments.

* **Keep active.** Stay connected with your normal life
as this will boost your self-confidence.

* **Combat depression.** If you feel depressed, contact
a counselor, therapist, or physician immediately.

Intentional Suicidal Ideations

Mental health care professionals relay that people commit
intentional suicide for about a handful of different reasons:
They are in desperate need of help and don't know how
to acquire it. They could have an underlying psychosis or
wish to end some sort of suffering or fear. They may have
been under the influence of drugs or alcohol. Or the most
common reason is they are severely depressed and believe
that being alive is just too demanding. However, I believe
that there is one other reason: spiritual interference.

Many years ago, my brother-in-law Joe, who was also
my best friend, passed away. Although sad, we accepted his
death, and I continued my pursuits. However, I kept hearing a voice coaxing me to take my life. It rationalized to me
that: "It is just like going to sleep. Only you won't wake up,
but you won't know it."

After realizing it was my brother-in-law who was
pestering me, I visited his grave and angrily told him to
leave me alone. I had no desire to die or be with him. As I

was starting to leave, an afterthought occurred about his unbearable girlfriend, so I returned to his grave.

Thoughts of his girlfriend Anna never helping us through the entire course of Joe's illness angered me. Thoughts of Anna refusing to attend Joe's funeral enraged me. Most importantly, immediately after Joe's death, Anna pursued my husband as well. She was despicable!

While this anger was totally consuming me, I screamed: "Joe, if you're lonely, take Anna with you. She's driving us all crazy, and she's better off with you. Just leave me alone!" After expressing these final words, I left and never turned back.

Within a week, Anna suddenly began missing Joe—which she had never expressed before. One week later, she was perpetually verbalizing her yearning to be with him. Six days after that, she committed suicide by rigging her car to fill with carbon monoxide and selfishly took her dog with her. Voices urging suicide never pursued me again.

In my career as a nurse for many decades, hundreds of patients have told me about feeling their deceased loved ones nearby and wishing to be reunited with them. Quite a few of those patients died under suspicious circumstances. It is not uncommon for the deceased to call on their loved ones. However, it also not uncommon for malevolent entities to trick people into committing suicide. If a person is consumed by desperation, fear, loneliness, or severe depression, they obviously have a lot of negativity surrounding them. Since negativity attracts the same, it is easy enough for a malevolent entity to pursue someone and trick them into taking their own life.

Whatever the reason, if you're suicidal, immediately call the National Suicide Prevention Hotline. If anyone you know is suicidal, call the hotline. *Always* take all suicide threats seriously! Only the victim knows the truth. Find out more at *SuicidePreventionLifeline.org*.

Saints Who Assist in Healing

Calling in saints can deter negative forces, but prior to asking for a saint's intercession, my clients are instructed to follow a couple of suggestions before initiating prayers and petitions.

First, obtain two white candles, preferably a five- or seven-day glass candle, which are also called "vigil candles." You can get such candles already dedicated to a particular saint, or you can place an image of the saint on the label or put your candle in front of a picture or a statue of the saint. Offer the saint a glass of fresh water. Light the candle, recite the appropriate prayer aloud, and introduce yourself. Suggest to the saint that they enjoy the candle and the fresh water. Leave the candle lit. Repeat this process every day, including offering a fresh glass of water daily—nobody likes stale water—until the candle is consumed.

The rationale behind lighting the first candle without a request is for the saint to become familiar with you and look favorably on you. For example, if you saw me on the street every day and each day I gave you a candy bar, you would not only look favorably upon me, but you would also be more apt to help me if I needed it.

If I were short on cash and needed three dollars for lunch, would you give me the money? Most likely you would because I have been the generous "candy lady." However, what if we had never met and I asked you for cash? Likelier than not, you would continue walking without acknowledging me. Of course, a saint would not be inclined to ignore our pleas, but the chances of successful manifestation of our requests are increased by familiarization.

The second and most important piece of advice for prayers and petitions is to speak with respect and humility. You are not "using" a saint—which is disrespectful in word and attitude. You are seeking help. Talk to the saint as if you are a child begging your parent for help. Be gracious and be grateful. Now, you are ready to light the second candle and ask for intercession.

St. Raphael, The Archangel

One of God's leading archangels, St. Raphael serves people who need to heal physically, mentally, emotionally, and spiritually.

Light a white candle to St. Raphael, and recite this prayer aloud. Before closing your prayer with the word *Amen*, repeat that you beg him to assist you with what is going on with your health problems. This may also be performed as a novena (from the Latin word for "nine"), reciting the prayer for nine consecutive days.

St. Raphael Prayer for Healing

Glorious Archangel, St. Raphael, great prince of the heavenly court, you are illustrious for your gifts of wisdom and grace. You are a guide of those who journey by land or sea or air, consoler of the afflicted, and refuge of sinners.

I beg you, assist me in all my needs and in all the sufferings of this life, as once you helped the young Tobias on his travels. Because you are the medicine of God, I humbly pray you to heal the many infirmities of my soul and the ills that afflict my body.

I especially ask of you the favor **(state your petition here)** and the great grace of purity to prepare me to be the temple of the Holy Spirit. Amen.

St. Dymphna

In life St. Dymphna faced persecution from her own father who had gone mad from grief when his wife died. We can turn to her now for help with emotional, mental, and nervous disorders.

Prayer to St. Dymphna

I turn to you, dear virgin and martyr, confident of your power with God and of your willingness to take my cause into your hands. I praise and bless the Lord for giving you to us as patron of the nervous and emotionally disturbed. I firmly hope that through your kind intercession He will restore my lost serenity and peace of mind. May He speak to my heart and reassure me: "My peace I give you. Let not your heart be troubled nor let it be afraid." Pray for me, dear St. Dymphna, that my nervous and emotional turmoil may cease, and that I may again know serenity and personal peace. **(State your particular petition here.)** Amen.

Other Saints Who Assist with Healing

Although there are numerous saints available to assist with healing, here are the most widely known saints in the Catholic as well as other spiritual traditions:

* **St. Rita:** Patron saint of victims of abuse, loneliness, body wounds, and ailments.

* **St. Lidwina:** Patron saint for those suffering from chronic illnesses.

* **St. Maximilian Kolbe:** Patron saint for those suffering from addictions.

* **St. Peregrine:** Patron saint for those suffering from cancer.

* **St. Jude Thaddeus:** Patron saint of desperate cases.

* **St. Lazarus the Leprous:** Patron saint of bone ailments, open wounds, and leprosy.

For a complete list of entities who help with specific illnesses as well as general miracle healers, see *Encyclopedia of Mystics, Saints & Sages: A Guide to Asking for Protection, Wealth, Happiness, and Everything Else!* by Judika Illes.

Making Promises to Saints

If you make a promise to a saint in exchange for the manifestation of your request, please fulfill that promise. Although a saint will not punish someone if the promise is not kept, future requests may not be fulfilled. To remind yourself of your promise, write it out on a piece of paper, then place it in the empty glass vigil container.

Caregivers Take the Rap!

Due to the financial greed of most health care delivery systems in the United States, failure to teach home caregivers what is direly needed for optimal recovery usually leaves everyone involved in a state of frustration and sometimes anger. Not only do they fail the families, but they severely fail the patients who are in their direct care. In fact, most of the institutionalized settings only deliver the physiological/medical necessities.

Health care providers are well aware that emotional wellness is connected to physiological wellness and essential for optimal recovery. However, due to understaffing, refusal by the insurance companies to provide anything that is nonreimbursable, and even the laziness of many "alleged" teachers, the industry severely fails the patients in direct care. You could even say things have regressed back to the levels of the Civil War era.

As both a registered nurse as well as a former administrator with a master's degree in health care administration, I can say from experience that all of this can't be placed at the feet of the insurance companies. Institutional greed laid the groundwork for where we are currently. However, now that the insurance companies have come out with rigid rules and regulations in an attempt to combat their having been taken advantage of in the past, it has provoked further financial cutbacks in health care industries to realize profits. As a result of all this financial wrangling, both patients and their caregivers suffer the consequences. Those helping infirmed loved ones at home have not been thoroughly instructed on what is direly needed for optimal recovery and those who work within institutions are helpless to improve existing conditions.

We've looked at the necessity of sunlight, fresh air, cleanliness, and positive sensory stimulation such as pleasant odors, sights, sounds, and the warmth of the human touch. We've also explored the human need for belonging. All people, and especially the elderly, need recognition and crave for their opinions to be valued. But unfortunately, clinical environments deprive patients of one, several, or all of these basic needs. Rooms are usually painted in drab institutional colors, and there may be unsightly clutter. The sounds are all mechanical and focused on monitoring the patient's functions. Sometimes, the odors of urine, feces, and/or blood, or the disinfectants to rid the space of the former are obnoxiously overwhelming. Sometimes windows are sealed shut, depriving the patient of fresh air. If the room is shared with another, it will be partitioned off with a curtain, further restricting the sense of space and sunlight. Unless the infirmed has frequent visitors, human contact is at a bare minimum, as health care providers do not have the time to prolong their interaction with them.

Furthermore, due to industry cutbacks, televisions and telephones are only provided to patients if they can afford the outrageously high prices charged. Many are restricted from walking around either because of a debilitating condition or due to institutional restrictions. That, in itself, deprives the infirmed of the ability to keep abreast of current events and communicate with others.

Many of these restrictive circumstances can also apply to care within the home unfortunately.

Obviously, almost every single human need is compromised, restricted, or withdrawn. It sounds worse than prison, doesn't it? Usually, the infirmed will first respond by seeking human interaction. Nurses will note the "perpetual call light" of a demanding patient. Caregivers at home may become overwhelmed by the number of times they are called to execute menial tasks the infirmed is perfectly capable of performing themselves. But the need for positive sensory stimulation first exhibits as attention-seeking actions. If solutions aren't found, then further problems will develop.

With the person under care suffering from the withdrawal of positive sensory stimuli, negativity now appears as its substitute. Anger and hostility will surface. Negative energy particles will be attracted to the infirmed, as if to a magnet. The anger, in turn, attracts more negative particles and begins to suppress the aura of the infirmed even more. If the caregiver isn't spiritually protected or psychologically prepared for these actions, they can sustain hurt, shock, anger, sadness, desperation, and/or other harmful feelings. Now, the negative particles are surrounding the caregiver too.

Next, the infirmed will begin to feel their suppressed aura and will interpret these sensations as impending doom, leading to fear. Fear is an intense stressor that activates our fight-or-flight response. Not only does this response compromise us physiologically as it sends all the body's defenses on high alert to counteract imminent attack, but it also forces us to perceive everything and everybody as a potential physical or mental threat to our existence. If the afflicted chooses to fight, the caregiver could face physical violence. By now, the infirmed probably has tears or holes in their aura, while the caregiver's aura will most likely have negative particle attachments. The caregiver may start to avoid the afflicted as much as possible out of a sense of self-preservation, which places this person in a state of near-isolation.

Isolation, in turn, becomes a welcome mat for malevolent spiritual entities because the infirmed is further mentally compromised and becomes desperate for any type of interaction. Any entity will usually appear as a friendly and understanding force who cares about the infirmed. Many times, these interactions are witnessed but misinterpreted as "talking to themselves."

The room of the infirmed—with all the negative particles and the presence of the malevolent entity—is now a spiritual "war zone." When you go in, you can literally feel sick from the noxious infestation of these energies.

The ultimate goal of the entity will be to take possession of the infirmed, just as a cancerous virus takes control of its host, in order to control the person, consume their life force to gain its own strength, and then abandon the deceased body and seek another victim. But first, it must protect its host from any threat to its own sustenance, and that means anyone or anything with the ability to return its host to a normal emotional or physiological state. (That's one of the reasons for frequent medical equipment failures.) If the host regains strength, the entity will be rejected and lose its nourishment. It will endeavor to control the infirmed by convincing them to resist any helpful actions others attempt with verbal abuse or insults. It can also try to fatigue the caregiver with constant outrageous demands.

If the caregiver is worn out or emotionally distraught from the victim's behaviors, the malevolent entity will also feed on this negativity. So the entire scenario becomes a "win-win" arena for the entity.

Therefore, it is crucial for caregivers to understand that any insults, outrageous demands, or slanderous and other undesirable behaviors are a cry for help from someone under the influence of a malevolent entity controlling these actions and words. The entity has gained power in the relationship. Although easier said than done, the caregiver must prepare to stay immune to these behaviors. Spiritual protection of both the patient and caregiver is imperative. Most importantly, measures must be implemented to repel the accumulation of negative forces.

Reducing the Amount of Negativity in a Patient's Room

5 empty votive candleholders, shot glasses, or any small container

Ammonia

Florida Water

1 square of camphor or an opened jar of Vicks Vaporub (which contains camphor)

A new pair of scissors

A Holy Bible

Using small cups or containers will offset both the odors and the awareness that spiritual work is being performed. Pour the ammonia into four of the votive cups. Place one cup in each corner of the room, being mindful that children or pets cannot enter the space unsupervised or they may knock the cups over.

Pour Florida Water into the last votive cup and add one square of camphor to this. Place it under the bed. If camphor is unavailable, continue with the Florida Water but also place the opened jar of the Vaporub under the bed.

Open the Bible to Psalm 121. This psalm protects people at night, especially when they are sleeping. It does not matter if the psalm is written on one page or on two, as the Bible must be opened.

Scissors have a number of uses within spiritual practices. One function is to repel negative entities. Place the opened scissors atop the open Bible with the blades of the scissor facing upward so that one blade and one handle of the scissors is over each page. Position this under the bed too.

Monitor the votive cups for evaporation and refill as needed.

Protection for the Caregiver

Wearing protective armor such as amulets, crystals, herbs, roots, and oils is just half the battle. As I have and will continue to remind my dear clients and readers: your magic must complement your behaviors, and your behaviors must complement your magic. Being armed with protection but continuing to show fear, anger, despair, and other negative emotions or thoughts will weaken your stance. It's almost akin to waving a loaded gun while running away from the perpetrator—the gun is useless! So a few behavioral changes will strengthen your position while weakening the negative forces:

* **Ignore all insults and false accusations.** Remaining calm, rather than any other reaction, will avoid

contributing additional negativity to the situation. Initially it may provoke further attempts to draw you out, but the undesirable behaviors will soon dissipate.

* **Meet demands with a smile on your face.** Again, this is easier said than done, but it is also a tried-and-true method that thousands of nurses have implemented successfully. Spending a little time with the patient and inquiring if more is needed will only confuse the negative forces.

* **Laugh.** Being cheerful and laughing is one of the most lethal weapons that a spiritual practitioner can carry. Negative forces detest laughter and cheerfulness because it weakens them. Usually, if these favorable behaviors are exhibited on an ongoing basis, it will become noticeable that the noxious ambiance of the room is gradually disintegrating.

Always remember that you are in combat with the negative forces and not the infirmed.

Return to Kindergarten

For over a decade, my dogs and I have trained in Schutzhund, a highly specialized dog sport that requires precise maneuvers from both the handler and dog. Often dogs falter in a previously mastered maneuver. When this happens, the coaches will always instruct the handler to "go back to kindergarten!" This means that, although frustrating, retraining a particular maneuver must be approached as if it were the dog's first encounter.

It later occurred to me that this concept applies not only to dogs, but to all humans in most areas of life as well. When we falter, we ought to go back to the beginning and start anew. The beauty of repeating a process is that we have now acquired wisdom in that given arena from our mistakes and will probably not falter again!

Once the negative forces have been weakened or dissipated, do not invite them back. We prevent reentry by implementing not only spiritual protection techniques but also by changing the factors that initially attracted them. So we go back to the beginning and:

* ⋆ Remove clutter.

* ⋆ Provide cleanliness of both the room and of the infirmed.

* ⋆ Provide sunlight and fresh air.

* ⋆ Provide appealing music and television programs.

* ⋆ Ensure that the infirmed feels needed and seek their opinions.

* ⋆ Avoid isolation and provide human interaction such as conversations.

* ⋆ Provide human touch such as hugs or hand-holding, as appropriate.

Unless the infirmed has been severely emotionally incapacitated, the techniques provided in this chapter ought to produce a marked improvement for both the infirmed and the caregiver.

6

Negative Spells, Curses, and Spells Gone Awry

Spells are magical maneuvers utilizing supernatural rituals designed to honor a spiritual entity or manipulate the outcome of an event and/or emotion. If the purpose of the ritual is to manipulate an outcome of an event or emotion, the spell is usually placed on either an object or a person. In some instances, spells may also be placed on animals either to directly affect them or use the animals as a means of transporting the spell to the intended place or person.

Negative Spells That Are Not Intended to Inflict Harm

Spellcasting is usually for positive or negative purposes. Negative spells are not always intended to inflict harm but instead to manipulate a situation in a forceful way. For instance, there are the spells from chapter 4, where a person may be binded/bound in order to prevent harm to others or placed in a mirror box, then frozen from preventing further damage. Other examples include:

* **Banishing spells:** To remove or dismiss unwanted people or conditions.

* **Breakup spells:** To remove someone from a relationship or a location. (In instances when breakup spells are cast to rescue a person from a toxic relationship, they are not considered a negative spell.)

* **Domination spells:** To gain control over another, usually in love or work relationships.

* **Hot foot spells:** To drive or send someone away.

* **Reversing spells:** To reflect curses back to the sender; a "return to sender" spell.

* **Tying the nature:** This popular Hoodoo practice is performed on a romantic partner in order to restrain that partner's sexual activities with others. In other words, these spells ensure fidelity.

Although such spells are not performed to inflict misfortune or harm on other people, they can indeed produce consequences, and the intended recipient, from here on in referred to as the "target," will feel as if something is out of the ordinary. The outcome of the spells and the effects they have on the target are all dependent on the knowledge, intent, and experience of the spellcaster. Let's discuss the noticeable effects that the target or an attentive observer may be able to detect.

Banishing Spells

With these least harmful of the "send-away" spells the target usually feels a sudden urge to depart from a place or person, never to return. An unexpected departure is highly indicative of spellwork. If the spell is performed by a kindhearted and experienced practitioner, the target may inexplicably receive great opportunities elsewhere.

Breakup Spells

Magic does not usually work overnight as it does on television. Its manifestation is gradual, but cumulative. With breakup spells what was once a harmonious relationship—with romantic or business partners, in friendships, and even for structures such as one's home or work environments—will begin to show signs of discord. Unresolved minor disagreements at the start could escalate and lead to further conflicts. There's usually confusion causing miscommunication. This results in a disinterest in the relationship, then avoidance, and finally repulsion for the place or person. The major sign and symptom that a spell is at work is if there is no rhyme or reason for the discord.

Domination Spells

When the target is fulfilling all the desires of one person with no consideration for themselves or others without question or pause, this is a major warning sign that a domination spell is in place. Other signs include being agreeable to all requests or thoughts of another, rewarding them for unearned achievements, a preoccupation for the person possibly presenting as an obsession, and/or a desire to be in the company of that person as much as possible.

Hot Foot Spells

Hot foot spells are another type of "send-away" spell usually involving forceable departure. Unlike banishing spells, in which there is a sudden urge to change locations, this spell delivers unexplainable conflicts that coerce one to flee.

Reversing Spells

Reversing spells are rituals performed when one wishes to turn a negative or harmful spell back to the sender. This is a defensive tactic that acts as a rubber mat to bounce harmful intent back to the sender. If a spellcaster finds intended harm to another affecting them instead, the target probably had a reversing spell in progress. I personally do not favor these spells because an inexperienced spellcaster ought not to engage in magical warfare with knowledgeable witches.

Tying the Nature

This spell involves dipping a string into the target's semen, which is then tied in knots while stating intentions aloud. Along with other curios, it is then placed in a small bag, called a "Nation Sack" and worn by the man's mate. Another version utilizes an effigy representing the penis, such as a penis figural candle, that can be preformed by a spellcaster. If a man is unable to obtain or maintain an erection for any woman other than one specific lover, this may be an indication that his nature may have been tied.

This is my least favorite spell as I have personally seen spellcasters perform it improperly causing the targets permanent impotence and, sometimes, penile cancer. Please do not perform this spell unless you have vast experience and knowledge of how to reverse it.

Curses

A curse is an expressed desire to cause harm, distress, or misfortune to another using supernatural force. Although there are distinct differences between the following options, curses are also commonly referred to as hexes, crossings, jinxes, maledictions, and whammies. Newer generations call it "throwing shade."

No matter the terminology, targets suffer from curses just as they would any other spell. Several ways to effectively execute a curse are through the use of:

* **Candle magic:** Burning candles in rituals is an effective means to facilitate one's desires. It is said that the flame of the candle pierces the veil between this world and the spiritual world, allowing us access to the entities on the other side. Additionally, the soothing and almost hypnotic effects of candle flames assist the spellcaster to concentrate and visualize the desired outcomes.

* **Effigies:** Anything that represents the target such as dolls, figural candles, pictures, etc. The aim is to create a link between the effigy and the target. If a personal concern is added to the effigy, such as the target's hair, nails, skin cells, saliva, or anything containing the target's DNA, the link becomes stronger.

* **Evil eye:** A targeted gaze given by the spellcaster accompanied by malicious thoughts, touch, and/or words.

* **Food:** Curses may be placed in food by either incorporating a nonpoisonous cursing ingredient into it or reciting incantations over it.

* **Foot track magic:** Casting a spell over or removing the impression of the target's footprint and mixing it with cursing ingredients and incantations make up an effective technique.

* **Laying or burying something on a path:** Sprinkling cursing ingredients, such as "Goofer Dust"

(a powerful cursing power), in the path of the target along with stating the intent that the target will be cursed upon making contact is a tried-and-true method. Cursing ingredients as well as cursed objects can also be buried along the path with the same stated intention.

★ **Objects:** As presented earlier in greater detail, an object is prepared and bewitched. Once the object is placed nearby and handled or stepped upon by the target, the curse is activated. This can include written intentions.

★ **Personal concerns:** When a spellcaster acquires anything that contains the target's DNA, it is easier to facilitate a link between the target and the intention.

★ **Pictures:** Also known as an adjunct to the body, pictures are clear representations of the target and can be utilized in almost any spell. However, the eyes of the target must be visible in the image.

★ **Pronouncement:** An authoritative verbal announcement or command of malediction. However, the statement must be made in the presence of the target to instill fear that results in self-harm.

★ **Spiritual entity assistance:** By summoning particular spiritual entities, the spellcaster may employ their supernatural powers to manifest the curse.

★ **Symbols:** There are many symbols in numerous spiritual paths representing the summoning of an entity along with a stated intention. These symbols are strategically placed in designated areas that are only known to an initiate of that given path.

Signs That You May Have Been Cursed

Before we list the signs suggestive of a curse, an analytical evaluation must first take place. There are a few points to deliberate prior to reaching the conclusion that you are the target of a curse.

First, consider a logical or mundane explanation for any mishaps you are having. For instance, if you are feeling fatigued, that could indicate a health problem, or if an electrical appliance breaks down, it might be a faulty or worn-out product.

Second, although it is not necessary to immediately identify the spellcaster, it is important to evaluate any reasons for a curse. Who would place a curse on you? Do you have enemies, adversaries, deceivers, or depressors lurking about? Has anyone been recently offended by your words or actions? Has anyone threatened you? Is someone enamored with your romantic partner or social or work status?

One of the major signs of a curse is when no matter how hard you attempt to overcome a challenge, you face continuous defeat. The obstacles presented sometimes seem both overpowering and overbearing. Curses are similar to mindless machines programmed to serve their functions without fail.

Last but not least, unless there is a life-threatening event, a one- or two-time occurrence of a mishap is usually not indicative of supernatural forces at play. These plaques are usually persistent and cumulative while lacking rational reasons for their happening.

Two or more of the following signs are usually in effect if you are under a curse:

* **Accidents:** Either a life-threatening or debilitating calamity might be indicative of a curse. However, a string of smaller accidents is usually the norm and will make one think, "Someone is out to get me."

* **Avoidance:** People, usually more than one, will suddenly begin to sidestep or shun you.

* **Apathy:** People are suddenly unemotional toward your misfortunes.

* **Appliance breakdowns:** Several appliances cease to work in a short period of time or electrical malfunctions occur.

* **Bad luck:** There is an ongoing run of bad luck.

* **Being watched:** There is a sense of being watched by an invisible negative force or entity.

* **Dismissal:** People no longer value your input or opinions.

* **Difficulty sleeping:** A sudden onset of insomnia, lacking precipitating causes, such as stress, anxiety, or having problem-solving decisions to make. Nightmares are often associated with this one.

* **Emotional variances:** Undesirable feelings, lacking a rational reason for their arousal, such as depression, anxiety, fear, restlessness, or even a sense of impending doom.

* **Fatigue:** There is an alteration in your normal daily activities caused by physiological interruptions of the need to rest or sleep. Sometimes, exhaustion is present with no discernible cause.

* **Financial difficulties:** There can be sudden and ongoing financial losses with the inability to recuperate or recover from the damage.

* **Generational curse:** A type of curse in which there are specified commands directed toward the target along with their offspring and all of their descendants. The calamities affecting each individual are of the same nature. This is a controversial topic

among spiritual practitioners. There are as many who believe it is possible as there are who do not.

* **Hag (night hag, hag riding):** Feeling the presence of a negative entity immobilizing you while sleeping. If this occurs, please see a physician immediately to ensure that it is not a physiological problem known as sleep paralysis instead.

* **Health problems:** Usually deteriorating in nature while physicians are unable identify the cause or diagnose the illness.

* **Insects:** Seeing or being approached by unusual insects not native to your area may indicate a curse. However, being attacked by many insects—whether foreign or not—may also signify being cursed. Insects appearing in swarms is also a warning sign of a curse. Lastly, if you see a vast amount of dead insects near you, it may indicate that they were directly affected by the malediction aimed toward you.

* **Jewelry:** Protective amulets or jewelry will "take a hit"—meaning they will shield you from the curse, taking it upon themselves, but then break from the tension.

* **Obstacles:** No matter what you try to do, it will seem like there is a brick wall preventing you from achieving your goals or desires.

* **Pets become ill:** As with protective jewelry, they too will "take the hit" for their owner.

Threats of a Curse

A very effective technique that many fraudulent spiritual practitioners employ is threatening to curse someone, although they never do. Instead they cleverly and effectively wait for the target's fear to produce self-injury. That fear suppresses the target's aura, sometimes producing holes and tears and leaving the aura susceptible to further injury or even attracting further calamities. Most of the time, the target will succumb to the con artist's demands in order to remove a curse that was never executed.

Most Curses Fade Away

Unless a spiritual entity has been summoned to hold a perpetual curse on the target—such as workings in a graveyard—the curse will eventually dissipate. As I have told hundreds of clients, if it is a case of a professional witch paid to perform the spells, their clients will not continuously pay for ongoing work. Additionally, if the spellcasters are not professionals but instead performing the spells themselves for personal reasons, most will eventually tire and let the work end.

Reverse the Curse?

When my clients are under curses, I always tell them not to engage in magical warfare as their first action, especially if they don't know who the sender of the curse is. I am not an advocate of reversing, or "return to sender," spells because if the source is a paid spellcaster with vast years of knowledge and experience, anything a novice attempts to do in retaliation could prove to be either futile or even fatal.

As a professional spellcaster, I will first assess a prospective client's situation prior to accepting a cursing case. The first point of business is to determine whether or not the cursing spell is justified. If I accept the case, by the time my spells are executed I have already assumed resentful emotions toward the target, and my anger is directed toward the injustices served to my client with the intent of delivering what the target deserves. In other words, "An eye for an eye, a tooth for a tooth . . ."

However, if the target has reversing spells in place, the energies directed toward them will be delivered back to me. With my vast years of experience, I can immediately sense and sometimes see the unwanted energies. As a psychic, I will be able to identify the culprit.

My first response is usually to laugh because it is amusing for a novice to dare attempt this with an expert. Then, there's irritation due to the additional burdens placed on me of yet another spiritual cleansing of myself, my pets, and my home. What happens next? Now it becomes personal! Not only am I upset that my client has been served injustices, but now I also have my own personal vendetta, and my spiritual retaliations are not pretty. That's the way it goes with professionals . . .

If, however, the spellcaster is a novice, and both caster and target have reversing spells in place, what happens then? It becomes an ongoing magical war until the energies finally dissipate. But during the process, time, energy, and money could be wasted on these spells.

Removing a Curse

First and foremost, do not panic! Fear is your own self-punishing enemy that weakens the aura while strengthening the negative forces. "Uncrossing"—a term used in Hoodoo for removing a curse—can be done successfully. However, your attitude, perseverance, and behaviors are essential for a favorable outcome.

Also keep in mind that being on the receiving end of a curse happens to the best of us and is not rare. Curses have been cast all around the world and since before the beginning of documented time. Therefore, if curses could not be removed, then misfortunes, calamities, and death rates would be a lot higher than what they are. Think of it this way: you're now a member of an elite, ancient group!

The second thing to remember is you are your own priority. Take care of yourself first and reserve your anger or need to retaliate for a later time. Obviously, frustration and disappointment are both natural and acceptable feelings, because you are now forced to engage in task-oriented chores taking up valuable time that could have been applied to other important endeavors. However, do not dwell on your frustrations, but instead, take the actions necessary to restore your spiritual well-being.

Now that you're focused on your priorities, make yourself a cup of nettle tea. Nettle (*Urtica dioica*), also known as stinging nettle, contains both spiritual as well as health values. The spiritual value offered by nettle is its uncrossing or jinx-breaking properties. It also contains certain nutrients that help to build our immune system, which will also benefit the aura. Now, sit down, relax, and drink your tea, then make your plan for removing the curse.

If you are a member of a spiritual or religious path, consult your leader as there are certain rituals sacred to given paths. Otherwise, follow these steps:

* **Step 1:** If you have a bewitched object, soak it in ammonia, then discard it.
* **Step 2:** Spiritually cleanse yourself.
* **Step 3:** Immediately don protective gear such as oils, Holy Water, or amulets.
* **Step 4:** Spiritually cleanse your dwelling.
* **Step 5:** Cleanse and rejuvenate the protection gear that is guarding your dwelling.

As frustrating as it is, you must "return to kindergarten" and start from the beginning in decontaminating yourself and your home. In most cases, though, these steps will remove the curse. If, however, the effects of the curse are still showing up, a stronger ritual, performed for thirteen days, will be necessary. For more on that eradication ritual see chapter 8.

Keep Silent

Frequently, the adversary will be watching their target to monitor the progress of the curse. If this enemy decides that the curse is not taking effect, they may perform additional cursing spells. But if the enemy believes that the target is suffering, they will focus on rejoicing over the agony they have caused. Sometimes, when the target is not accessible, the enemy will trick an innocent friend or relative into relaying an account of their target's well-being.

Therefore, it is best to keep a low-profile. Do not speak of the curse or any of the effects that the curse has had on you, such as lack of sleep or bad luck. Once the curse has been removed, do not rejoice in your happiness or well-being, which may also provoke the spellcaster to perform additional curses. The best piece of advice I can give everyone is to keep silent and act as if nothing ever happened. In many cases—but not all—the spellcaster will lose interest in future spells due to the ambiguity of the spell's effect. Remember: silence is golden!

Open the Roads

Once the curse has been removed, it may be necessary to do some damage control by reopening any doors that were closed by it. In Hoodoo, we call this opening the roads, doors, or gates. For instance, you may wish to open the roads for relationship or job opportunities to come forward. A few suggestions for road-opening rituals are listed below. All of them are equally effective. Start your ritual on a Monday during the waxing moon phase.

Road Opener 1

Purchase a Road Opener glass-encased candle. Starting on a Monday, place a picture of yourself—with your eyes showing!—faceup, on a fireproof surface, and then put the candle directly on the picture. Recite the following Road-Opening Prayer every day and ensure that your petition remains consistent each day. Do not change your requests.

Road-Opening Prayer

I invoke the sublime influence of the eternal father to obtain success in all the subjects of my life and to smooth all difficulties that are in my way. I invoke the aid of the Holy Spirit so that my house prospers and my company and my person receive a message of good luck sent by the Divine Providence. Oh great hidden power, I implore your supreme majesty so that you separate me from danger, at the precise moment, that my way is illuminated by the light of fortune. I shall receive the infinite blessing of the sky. (*State your petition*) I believe in God, all powerful Father. Amen!

Road Opener 2

Obtain a nine-inch orange candle and cleanse it with salt water or Florida Water. With a pencil inscribe on it from bottom to top in script, nine times: "Open the Roads." Do not lift your pencil as you fill in this message from the bottom to the top of the candle.

On a Monday, anoint the candle with either Road-Opening Oil or olive oil. Immediately roll it in either dried crushed *abre camino* herb or a Road-Opening Incense, which may be found in spiritual supply stores both on- and offline. Place a picture of yourself—with your eyes show-ing!—faceup inside a glass candleholder. Then place the candleholder on a fireproof surface. Set the candle directly on the picture. Recite the Road-Opening Prayer every day and ensure that your petition remains consistent each day. Despite what the product websites state, nine-inch candles burn for a period of 28–32 hours.

When the candle has extinguished itself, bury the wax and your picture either in your front yard or inside a potted houseplant. If neither are an option, bury it near a consent-ing tree and ask that as the tree grows, so will your opportu-nities. Thank the tree, and pay it for its services by burying a dime next to it and offering it fresh water to drink.

Road Opener 3

This ritual has helped many of my clients achieve what had appeared to be impossible tasks. One client was homeless, living in her car. After petitioning St. Peter, she's now the manager of one of the poshest restaurants in California.

Another client, living alone, jobless, and without a romantic relationship in over ten years, was in a state of despair. After performing this ritual, she is now a happily married and semi-famous journalist traveling all around the world!

The secrets to achieving success with this ritual are twofold. The first challenge is that it takes months to man-ifest. Therefore, you must remain patient and have faith that St. Peter will grant your petition. Sometimes, I ques-tion whether or not he is purposely testing our faith. The second challenge—as with all holy deities—is that you must approach him with humbleness, respect, and humility. Speak to St. Peter as a child speaks to its parent.

St. Peter was an Apostle of Jesus Christ. Because of his faith and loyalty to Jesus, St. Peter was imprisoned by

King Herod. But an angel came with the key to unlock the prison door and set him free. Now St. Peter holds the keys to the Pearly Gates of Heaven and is associated with unlocking all doors and opening all roads.

Obtain two glass-encased St. Peter vigil candles. On a Monday, place a picture of yourself—with your eyes showing!—faceup on a fireproof surface, and then set one candle directly on the picture.

Do not ask any favors of St. Peter. This is just a preliminary getting acquainted ritual. Light the candle and recite the following prayer aloud every day.

Prayer to St. Peter

O Holy Apostle, because you are the Rock upon which Almighty God has built His Church, obtain for me I pray you: lively faith, firm hope, and burning love, complete detachment from myself, contempt of the world, patience in adversity, humility in prosperity, recollection in prayer, purity of heart, a right intention in all my works, diligence in fulfilling the duties of my state of life, constancy in my resolutions, resignation to the will of God, and perseverance in the grace of God even unto death; that so, by means of your intercession and your glorious merits, I may be made worthy to appear before the Chief and Eternal Shepherd of Souls, Jesus Christ, Who with the Father and the Holy Spirit, lives and reigns forever. Amen.

Offer St. Peter a glass of fresh water. Introduce yourself and suggest that he enjoy the candle and the fresh water. Leave the candle lit. Every day, repeat this process, including offering a fresh glass of water daily—nobody likes stale water—until the candle is consumed.

Wait until the following Monday to begin your petition.

On the following Monday, place a picture of yourself—
with your eyes showing!—faceup on a fireproof surface,
and then set the second candle directly on the picture.
Recite the Prayer to St. Peter aloud, but before closing with
Amen, ask your requests. Remember to recite your prayer
daily and keep the request/petition constant and consistent. Also offer fresh water every day.

If you make a promise to St. Peter for granting your
request, please fulfill that promise. Saints will not punish
someone if a promise is not kept; however, if future
requests are made, they may not be answered. To remind
yourself of your promise, write it out on a piece of paper,
then place it in the empty glass vigil container.

Seek Revenge or Walk Away?

Once my clients have been completely released from a
curse and opportunities are being presented, they usually
forget about the malicious intent toward them. Instead
they decide that life is too precious as well as too short to
waste their time seeking revenge on the spellcasters.

However, there are many who cannot forget or forgive
the pain and anguish imposed on them. The ones who can't
forget are usually astrological fire signs. As an Aries, I can
relate to those very sentiments! Whether you decide to walk
away or seek magical revenge, do what feels right for you.

If you make the decision to seek magical revenge, be
sure that you, your home, and your loved ones, such as
children and pets, are protected. Without protection, the
energies associated with negative spells can also attach
themselves to those who are unguarded. Also, ensure that
you spiritually clean yourself and your home after the spell
has been executed.

Most importantly, wait for your revenge. Letting some
time elapse is good for three reasons: The enemy will be off

guard. It provides space for excellent planning. Revenge is a dish served best cold.

Spells That Have Gone Awry

There have been thousands of novice spellcasters seeking my help believing that their spells had "backfired" because either the intent of the spells had also affected the magician or there were severe repercussions inflicted on innocent people during the manifestation of the spells. But spells do not backfire on people. The consequences they were seeing were due to the omission of certain precautions that the experienced magician always takes into consideration during the planning phase of their work.

When the Spell Affects the Magician

The most common complaints I've heard are about spells that either lead the spellcaster to instead experience an amplification of their love for their target in the case of love spells or a run of bad luck after performing a darker form of magic. These effects can be easily prevented.

While casting a spell, always remember that numerous forms of energy are being both summoned and manifested. The spellcaster is positioned directly in the middle of these energies in what I like to call "being in the direct line of fire." Therefore, whether casting positive or darker forms of magic, the magician will feel the effects if they haven't taken the proper preventative steps. Furthermore, as we have previously discussed, energies will attach not only to living beings but also to objects.

Prior to casting a spell, first spiritually cleanse yourself to remove any debris on your skin that may act as a barrier between your protection measures and your aura. Next, do the same with your workspace and remember to remove any clutter. Then, implement as many protection methods as possible to safeguard yourself in the line of fire. When the spell has been completed, again cleanse yourself and your workspace to remove any residual energies.

The Repercussions of Positive or Negative Magic

I have two sample cases that, with the permission of my clients, I have relayed to hundreds of people about being too emotional while casting a spell and therefore neglecting to scrupulously review commands and petitions. The spoken word has unthinkable power, and therefore, one must reason through what will be said (and written) when implementing spells.

Case 1

The loving wife and mother of two young children had no idea that her husband was unhappy in their marriage. Without warning, he moved out of the house and into the arms, and home, of another woman.

The wife, still in love with her husband, desperately wanted him back. She therefore resorted to spellwork. Being a novice, she purchased a love-spell kit and followed the manufacturer's instructions to the letter for the physical preparations of the spell. However, no instructions were provided for her verbal commands.

Unfortunately, during the spell she stated several times that: "Jim will come back at all cost." She failed to consider that it was a love-spell kit and didn't think about manipulating his emotions by stating something like Jim would miss her and fall in love with her again. Instead, she erroneously commanded an action by stating just *that he would come back* and, most dangerously, neglected to consider the consequences of the words *at all cost.*

One day, she was preparing to take her children shopping, but found she had forgotten her keys. She momentarily left the children outside to run back into the house. In that instant, her three-year-old daughter ran into the street and was killed by a passing car. Jim came back to help her with funeral arrangements and to mourn. Sadly, her spell manifested exactly as she had commanded, but the cost was the life of her child. To this day, she is grief-stricken.

Case 2

The boyfriend of one of my beloved clients broke up with her after an argument. She assumed that he would return to her, as he always did, after they argued. Instead, he fell deeply in love with another woman who neither had knowledge of his prior relationships nor of my client's existence. She was an innocent soul and appeared to be a good person.

Although my client did not wish to revive a relationship with this man, she implemented a breakup spell out of revenge. Her intention was for him to feel the exact emotional pain that he had caused her. However, out of anger and not realizing the potential consequences of her commands, she petitioned that the breakup would produce enduring and agonizing emotional torment.

Her breakup spell manifested as her ex-boyfriend found his new girlfriend on his bed deceased. As a result, he experienced the exact enduring and agonizing emotional torment my client had asked for. My client was also devastated and sustained guilt, shame, and self-persecution, for it had not been her intention to cause the death of an innocent person.

Protect the Innocent

Clearly, we have to be careful because magic can produce *exactly what we ask for*, and without proper planning, we won't be able to see all the consequences a spell could manifest. All stated and verbal commands must be painstakingly scrutinized to ensure that innocent people are not harmed.

The Wiccans have a beautiful code of honor, which is the conclusion of their Rede: "An Ye Harm None, Do What Ye Will." Although I am not a Wiccan, these words always remind me to include a verbal statement in my commands ensuring that innocent people are not affected by any of my spells. Usually I'll conclude my command with the words "without harm to others."

Prevent Being a Casualty of Another's Casual Spellwork

Unfortunately, even if you are not the target of a spell nor have any known enemies, you can still be afflicted by the potency of another's magic. In other words, you can innocently find yourself in the "direct line of fire" if you have an association with the target or you come into direct contact with a spell, such as stepping on a cursing powder meant for someone else or handling a bewitched object.

That's why spiritual protections ought to be maintained at all times. The best line of defense is the direct application of protective gear on your body, such as oils, waters, amulets, and other methods previously discussed in chapter 1. Yet sometimes we may falter with the consistent practice of our daily protection routine. Having a secondary line of defense is prudent in the event that you have indeed faltered, but keep in mind that no method is as powerful as those that are in direct contact with the body and aura.

Reverse Mirror Box Spell for Protection

Two-inch or four-inch square mirrors can be purchased at almost any craft store and are usually sold in packets of four. You will need six mirrors. Make a cardboard box of the same size as the mirrors but do not seal the top of the box until the contents are placed inside.

Place a picture of yourself, with eyes showing, inside the box along with your personal concerns such as hair, fingernails, skin cells, blood, etc. Now fill the box completely with the herb rue. Pray Psalm 23 over the box and ask God and the spirits of the herbs to protect you.

Seal the box with the last piece of cardboard, then tape up the box completely. With the reflective side of the mirrors facing outward to deflect any negative energies coming toward you, take the mirrors and glue one mirror to each side of the box. Protection oil may be applied to the mirrors. Keep this in a safe place, such as under your bed. Replace with a new box yearly.

7

Harmful Spiritual Entities

S piritual entities are supernatural beings that often-
times, but not always, exist outside of a physical body.
These entities are present all around us, in many forms,
and serve different functions. Entities can be helpful, such
as revered deities we summon when in need of support or
our Spirit Guides and Guardian Angels, serving to aid us in
fulfilling our life mission.

Conversely, some spiritual entities can be mischievous,
showing a playful desire to cause trouble, while others can
be downright wicked and malicious, parasitically serving
to meet their own agendas while damaging the well-being
of others. Moreover, just like humans, several forms of
spiritual entities can be either good or evil.

The spiritual entities I have encountered in my life,
either through my own personal experiences or those of
my clients, that may serve in a harmful capacity are:

* **Angels:** Although widely considered to be agents
  of God, there are also entities referred to as angels
  that actually work within a demonic capacity, such

as many of the "fallen angels" who were expelled from heaven.

* **Demons:** Evil or malevolent entities. Most commonly thought of as agents from Hell.

* **Djinn (jinn, genies):** Magical creatures, believed to have been created by fire or smoke, with the capacity to appear in human or animal form. They have free will and possess the ability to influence humankind toward either good or evil—depending on their nature.

* **Elementals:** Magical entities possessing the power or the force of nature in which they reside. These include gnomes residing in the element of earth, undines residing in the element of water, sylphs residing in the element of air, and salamanders residing in fire.

* **Fairies:** A form of spirit described as human in appearance but varying in size from miniature to that of a small human child. Fairies can be helpful, neutral, or harmful to humans.

* **Ghosts:** With various descriptions and definitions, these are the souls of people or animals that are earthbound. They have unfinished business, do not wish to cross over to the spiritual realm, are confused, or have obstacles preventing them from crossing over.

* **Gods or Goddesses:** Revered deities who may cause harm if they're summoned and do not wish to be. Another concern is if the deity requires a specified sacrifice when a petition is granted because if the petitioner is not aware of that required sacrifice, such as blood, the deity may just take it anyway and in the harshest manner. . . .

* **Sleep demons:** Those that usually attack people at night, usually while asleep. The most common of these entities are:
  * **Hags:** Nightmare demonic witches or spirits, capable of shape-shifting, appearing as ugly old women that immobilize a sleeping person.
  * **Incubi:** Demonic entities appearing male that lie upon sleeping women for sexual activity.
  * **Succubi:** Demonic entities appearing as females that lie upon sleeping men for sexual activity.
* **Wild spirits:** This category consists of trolls, goblins, nixies, sirens, and imps. They ought to be treated as one would a wild animal because their behaviors are unpredictable.

This list is solely a brief classification of the thousands of existing spiritual entities. For a comprehensive classification, I highly recommend the book *Encyclopedia of Spirits: The Ultimate Guide to the Magic of Fairies, Genies, Demons, Ghosts, Gods and Goddesses* by Judika Illes.

Attracting Negative Entities

Most of us, at one time or another, have inadvertently summoned a negative entity without even realizing it. If we are physiologically and emotionally healthy, we will also possess a strong and vibrant aura that will immediately deter the unwanted visitors from prolonging their stopover. In such an event, we might never have been aware of their presence.

However, when we are in a weakened state of body, mind, or spirit, we become vulnerable and attract their attentions. Other situations that pique their interests are if we summon them, unknowingly extend an invitation to them, or have an association with other entities while neglecting to enforce the proper measures to filter out unwanted ones—in other words, they will view your association with other entities as an "open door policy."

Unless someone has purposely summoned a negative entity—and many masterfully do so within a controlled environment—the greatest number of cases involving visitations from them are due to illness, which weakens the mind, body, and aura; a lack of knowledge; and, sadly, acts of desperation. Hopefully, this chapter will provide the information needed to understand what circumstances attract these entities and how to minimize unwanted contact.

Alcohol Withdrawal and Delirium Tremens (D.T.'s)

An addict who stops consuming alcohol will sometimes suffer from delirium tremens (d.t.'s), a severe form of withdrawal, around three days after the last intake of alcohol. The visible signs of d.t.'s consist of tremors, shivering, profuse sweating, elevated temperature, vomiting, seizures, and other events. Many report seeing snakes, rats, and other animals of various colors. While I was in nursing school, our most scientific-oriented instructor once said: "If everybody is seeing the exact same things, there must be a dimension in existence that antagonizes victims."

Answering Something Calling Your Name

My mother used to frequently warn me that if an unrecognizable voice calls my name, do not answer! Unwanted entities look for invitations and rely on an affirmative answer, such as your unknowingly responding "yes" to such a call. Instead, walk up to whoever you believe is calling. If you are home alone, shout: "Go away, you are not welcomed in my home!" Then, recite a protection prayer, of your choice, aloud.

As the years have gone by, this exact same warning was issued to me from numerous spiritual practitioners of various faiths, religions, and ages. Finally, I actually experienced this situation. It sounded as if I were being called by someone on the opposite side of a closed door—which was actually the veil separating our world from the spiritual realm.

Answering Something Knocking at Your Door

Because entities seek invitations, my mother also warned me that if there's a knock at the door, never open it without first seeing who it is or asking aloud if there's no peephole. A door opened wide may be viewed as a welcome. If you find nobody is on the other side, once again shout: "Go away, you are not welcomed in my home!" Then, recite a prayer aloud.

Although no one has ever mentioned this to me, welcome mats always make me suspicious. Are they possibly inviting negative entities? Maybe I'm overly cautious here, but it's better to be safe than sorry!

Approaching an Unknown Entity

When exploring the outdoors, we may sometimes see either elementals or fairies going about their business. Just as humans would, they may glance at us before continuing what they were doing, be appalled by our presence, or become angry. I once saw a fairy working who stopped what he was doing and stared, clearly irritated with me. Once I walked away, he returned to his work. If you see these entities, ignore them and walk away. This advice applies to all types of entities.

Bones and Body Parts of Deceased Animals or People

The spirits of animals or people usually attach themselves to their body parts, especially if they have lost their lives in an inhumane manner. Unless you are well aware of the manner in which the "owners" of the bones passed away, it is unwise to keep them in your possession. Their spirits may cause great grief or even harm to the handler. The exception to this is if you know how to release the spirit.

Calling on an Unknown Entity

Never call on any entity unless you are fully aware of who and what they are, what they require, their history, and with whom they associate. The three most common errors among clients who have sought my help after having contacted an unknown entity and then suffered the consequences thereafter, are the following:

* **Misusing Ouija boards:** People are under the misconception that these boards attract negative entities. It is not the Ouija board; rather it is the act of verbally summoning unknowns.

* **People summoning aloud using the wording "I call on anybody who will help me":** This is a huge mistake because it offers an invitation to *any* entity, and of course, they will respond under the guise of being helpful ones.

* **Reciting prayers in an unknown language:** Unless you understand exactly what you are saying, do not recite something. Additionally, don't take someone else's interpretation as your basis for action either—as I personally learned the hard way. Once a Greek boy said he would teach me how to

greet my father in his language. Instead, he taught me sexually explicit words for which I was severely punished! Research the words on your own, for they may be of a harmful nature.

Curses: Delivering or Receiving Them

Many curses are worked together with malicious entities who assist the spellcaster. Novice practitioners ought not perform these types of spells alongside impish entities unless there is direct, hands-on supervision from an experienced mentor. Otherwise, the entity may decide to remain with the spellcaster and cause havoc.

On the receiving end of a curse, the entity will most likely frequently visit or remain with the target. It all depends on the commands of the spellcaster.

Death

Anyone visiting graveyards without any spiritual protection may attract an entity who will attach to that person. In Santería, I was taught that entities attach themselves to the crown of the head and/or the back of the neck. Therefore, those areas ought to be protected prior to entering a graveyard/cemetery.

During my time as both a combat and level-one trauma nurse, hundreds of patients have died in my presence. It has been my observation that those who have passed on laying on their right side had loving family members surrounding them, whereas those who have passed lying on their left side were frequently of questionable character.

Spiritual practitioners have warned me that those laying on their left side were the ones most likely to become ghosts and attach themselves to the living if spiritual protection is not in place.

Drug Addiction

As with any emotional and physiological illness, the body, mind, spirit, and aura are severely weakened and compromised with drug addiction. In addition to the usual ramifications of illness, there is often a desperate need for more drugs. These combined states serve as a welcome mat for malicious entities that sometimes do convince their victims to perform evil acts.

Evil Assaults on Others

Antisocial personalities are most apt to perform heinous crimes and acts such as torture, sexual trafficking, forced labor, rape, disfigurements, sexual mutilation, and killings—including serial killings and mass murders. These hateful and reprehensible crimes are carried out by evil people. Evil people attract the same, in both human and spiritual form. Their demeanors toward their hateful deeds are frequently apathetic, and they do not display any emotions of remorse or guilt.

Evil begets evil and these people are usually closely associated with malicious entities serving as their advisors, assistants, and sometimes protectors. Usually, they appear to be in at least a partial state of entity possession as we can frequently observe in their bulging eyes and monotone voices. Professional rehabilitation does not focus on the spiritual causation of their behaviors, and therefore, attempts at restoring a victim to normalcy are often in vain.

The best advice is to avoid these people at all cost. Many have tried to show kindness and were paid back with severe disfigurements or even the loss of their lives. Also, any attempt by a nonprofessional to display concern could attract the evil entity to you because kindness is viewed as weakness.

Feeding Unknown Entities

Never provide nourishment—such as food, water, or candles—to an unknown entity. It only gives them strength, as it would for a living creature.

One time a client had consulted with an inept rootworker seeking advice for her ten-year-old daughter who was speaking to an entity named John. The name John, by the way, is the first indication that this might be a demonic entity, because they lie about their names and invent those that are simple and common. John's face was so dark that it was barely visible, while his garb was a black robe. John did not like to pray or talk about God either, but he maintained a friendly rapport with the child. The child, in turn, relayed daily accounts of her encounters and conversations with John to this concerned mother.

That rootworker erroneously advised her that, because this entity's name was John, he must be one of the Apostles. The rootworker advised the mother to offer the entity fresh water, bread, and a lit candle on a daily basis in order to give him strength. And, so she did . . .

John was now welcomed by both the child and her mother. Then, John asked the child to invite another of his "Spirit Friends," and the child consented. There were now two invited entities in the house who were strengthened with nourishment and treated as if they were family. But this was also when the perpetual run of bad luck struck everyone living in that house. When John asked to have a third spirit invited, the mother became worried and contacted me.

The circumstances relayed to me indicated profound malevolence, and the reading showed that they were of a demonic source. As I was unable to travel to her location, we contacted a local Native American shaman who successfully exorcised the entities. Upon leaving, the shaman stated that the nourishment provided to these entities could have potentially opened a floodgate of evil. I then coached my client to spiritually cleanse each person living in the home, then cleanse the house, followed by protection measures for all the people living in the home as well as the home itself. The family has lived in peace ever since.

Floodgates

When people begin communicating with spirits, more often than not without strict supervision and training, it both relays a message to the spirit world that there is someone capable of communication and leaves a door wide opened for other entities to enter the communicator's space. It is akin to a store having a one-day super sale and, when they open the doors for the event, they become a virtual floodgate as swarms of people rush in.

When watching movies, I frequently admire scriptwriters for their astonishing research into the subject. There is a scene in the fictional movie *Ghost* that comes to mind as an example of the consequences of untrained people communicating with spiritual entities.

In the movie, once the incompetent and fraudulent psychic medium Oda Mae Brown is contacted by a real ghost and she answers him, the message immediately goes around the spirit world of a new communicator being onboard. Suddenly she has a never-ending crowd of spirits feverishly competing with one another to have her attention. She is practically inundated by them!

This scenario can also transpire in real life. Unfortunately, if the neophyte medium cannot adeptly control who visits and when the visitations are allowed, these entities will perpetually pester them, causing sleep deprivation and, eventually, losing the thread of reality in this world. Additionally, any type of spiritual entity can—and will—visit.

If you have been contacted by an entity and are not properly trained to control the situation, please consult an expert on the matter rather than continuing the interactions. Don't take the entity's word of who it is or what it wants at face value because negative entities are liars that work through deception.

Illnesses

As we've previously discussed in great detail, negative entities are attracted to those who are plagued with physiological and/or emotional dis-ease.

Intranquil Spirit

This entity originates from the Mexican spiritualist and *Brujería* traditions and has become very popular among numerous Hoodoo practitioners and followers. People summon this spirit in order to torment a lost lover until they return to the petitioner.

There are varying beliefs as to what this spirit actually is and where it resides. Opinions range from it being one to numerous spirits, residing in either Hell or Purgatory. Others believe that such intranquil spirits are earthbound ghosts of deceased who were once evil. Those who believe that it is one spirit sometimes associate it with the Lonely Spirit ("Anima Sola") who resides in Purgatory or even with Santisima Muerte ("Most Holy Death").

Whatever it is, here is the bottom line: this is an unknown entity whose origins are also unclear. Working with this entity is taking a big risk because people have reported that afterward they have been either tricked by it or even suffered consequences. Unless you're an expert at controlling this entity, it is wise to avoid it. There are hundreds of love spells in numerous spiritual traditions that don't require such risk-taking.

Invitations

Herein lies one of the most—if not *the* most—important objectives of this chapter and, therefore, worthy of repetition: *do not invite any unknown spiritual entities into your life or your home!* If you are not 100 percent certain of its identity, then avoid it until more information can be gathered.

In her book *Encyclopedia of Spirits,* author Judika Illes writes that "it is easier to invite them in than to make them leave." Always remember that a moment of vulnerability can result in an unbelievable amount of hardship caused by the havoc they can create and all of the work and effort it takes to get rid of them.

Loneliness

Some folks are fortunate enough to feel happy alone and are grateful for the freedom to independently go anywhere they wish and to do anything that they please while never having to worry about accountability. Conversely, depending on culture and/or upbringing, others who are alone instead feel loneliness, which is defined as a depressing feeling, destitute of sympathetic or friendly companionship, intercourse, support, etc.

If emotions of loneliness are prolonged, they can ultimately set the foundation for desperation, and negative entities are always on the lookout for people in this state of mind. Also if one feels deprived of sexual pleasures, sexual demons, such as incubi or succubi, will attempt to fulfill these needs, while causing harm to their victims by draining them of their vital forces.

If you feel lonely, attempt to find stimuli that will preoccupy you from experiencing these emotions by seeking out social events or using social media, television, or pet ownership to change your mind-set. Most importantly, do not accept any social advances from entities.

Participating in Unknown Rituals or Ceremonies

If you are invited to participate in any sort of spiritual ritual, always ensure that you have a full grasp of what th ritual entails, who or what is being summoned, and the reason for the event. Do not take the ritual leaders' words with blind faith, as those with ulterior motives can be both charming and convincing. Ask as many questions as possible, including the reason for your invitation. Most importantly, if you have any reservations or feelings of doubt about a ceremony, *do not participate.* First impressions and gut instinct are means our Spirit Guides and/ or Guardian Angels use to attempt to warn us, so trust these feelings.

There was once a client who had been plagued by ongoing negative occurrences. Although she was seeking my help to eradicate these tormenting events, her behaviors were suspicious, and I felt she was attempting to protect something or someone. During our lengthy phone interview, there were times when she genuinely pleaded for help while still evading particular questions. These behavioral oddities suggested to me that she feared retaliation.

Of particular note were the consistent technological interferences and disruptions with both of our phone lines. Despite the incredible obstacles presented during this conversation, it appeared that this woman was actively in the first stage of demonic possession.

It took two painstaking hours of questioning to finally identify the initial encounter. She had succumbed to peer pressure by participating in an event called "A Demonic Tea Ceremony." Although I am unfamiliar with such rituals or the ceremonial details, it was nevertheless clearly the onset of her ongoing difficulties and when a demonic entity attached itself to her. On that day she had unknowingly sacrificed her well-being for fear of being abandoned by her friends. Ironically, once her troubles started, these "friends" ultimately abandoned her anyway. Sadly, it was a "lose-lose" scenario for this poor lady . . .

Also, be wary of any events alluding to sexual encounters. Usually, the names used include terms such as *erotic*. If you do seek out these encounters, please ensure that the person conducting the event has vast years of experience. Erotic séances can summon both incubi, demonic entities appearing male that lie upon sleeping women for sexual activity, and succubi, demonic entities appearing female that lie upon sleeping men for sexual activity, and their presence, if uncontrolled, can produce dire repercussions. Erotic hypnosis can produce the same results. Additionally, if you participate in any hypnotic events, ensure that the hypnotist holds a license to conduct hypnotherapy.

Most importantly, confirm that these rituals are not being conducted to solely satisfy the sexual desires of the leaders. Often services offered under the guise of "spiritual assistance" can be another form of sexual predation.

Possessed Objects

An object can be possessed voluntarily or through an involuntary binding, and the means of that possession are not for you to ascertain or diagnose. If you see vast changes in the behaviors of anyone, including animals, after introducing a different object into the household, it might be possessed. Other signs to look for are visual or auditory insults. See chapter 3 for in-depth details.

Summoning Unknown Gods, Goddesses, Demigods, Angels, and Saints

Most people naively associate Gods, Goddesses, angels, and saints with the holiest entities presiding in Heaven, loving all humankind and watching over us to ensure our well-being to the best of their abilities. In actuality, there are hundreds—if not thousands—of different entities that have existed or still do exist all around the world ruling over varying domains.

Gods and Goddesses

These entities have been worshipped by the ancient Egyptians, Mesopotamians, Greeks, Hindus, Norse, etc., virtually since the beginning of time. There are Supreme Gods, Mother of Gods, Father of Gods, gods with animal features, Sun Gods and Moon Gods, Star Gods, Elemental Gods, Weather Gods, and on and on. Reading a short article about a particular god or goddess does not provide the vast knowledge required to work with one of them because their histories, temperaments, and requirements vastly differ. Unless you have been raised in the culture ruled by a particular god or goddess or you are an extremely knowledgeable Pagan with years of experience, it is advisable to avoid petitioning them because the repercussions may be harsh penalties.

There was once a neophyte Pagan who reawakened and summoned an ancient god for monetary wealth. His petition was granted; however, he was unaware that this particular god required a blood sacrifice for payment. When the neophyte failed to pay the god for his services, the god instead took it upon himself to collect his due. The neophyte lost both of his arms in an accident. The cost far exceeded his monetary gain.

I also knew a neophyte Pagan who lost his life in a fire after he had awakened and petitioned a particular fire god, then failed to provide proper payment. There have been various accounts of drownings and other casualties due to the same. It is just a good policy to only petition an entity with whom you are completely familiar.

Demigods

These are minor deities who are the offspring of a god or goddess and a human. Popular well-known demigods would include Hercules, Romulus, Remus, and Perseus, who successfully killed Medusa, the monster with snakes in place of her hair. It is said that many demigods become enraged if summoned.

Saints

Saints exist in many traditions and not solely the Catholic or Christian religions. As with other deities, proceed with caution.

Angels

Beware of fallen angels and those demonic entities who are addressed as angels.

Talking to Yourself

Lonely people, the elderly, and those with alterations in their psychological stability may exhibit the habit of talking to themselves. This conduct is an invitation for conversations with entities. The observable behaviors will consist of initial self-soothing speech. Once an entity is present, the victim will receive answers only audible to them. This is followed by the victim engaging in intense conversations, and finally, the victim will prefer the company of the entity rather than human interaction.

Softly correct these behaviors in the initial phases. Inform the person what could result from these self-soothing behaviors. Offer something to preoccupy the person, such as television, chores to accomplish, etc., in order to keep them from harm.

Vision Quests

Popularly associated with Native American traditions, a vision quest is an ongoing search for the meaning and purpose of life and the pursuit of spiritual enlightenment. These quests have been undertaken by people from all over the world for centuries. Notable biblical figures, the Buddha, mystics, and millions of others have successfully achieved their goals of enlightenment after having engaged in vision quests. Unfortunately, others have been unable to overcome the barriers or obstacles along their paths.

One of the most common obstacles people on these quests encounter is self-induced confusion due to a lack of focus. Instead of remaining devoted to their initial pursuits, they either deviate from the first path upon receiving new or different information or they attempt to incorporate all the information simultaneously.

This often reminds me of an acquaintance who had initially sought to learn the African Derivative Tradition (ADT) of Hoodoo because she believed it to be her path. Within two months of studying Hoodoo, she also began practicing Santería. A few months after that, her practices also incorporated both Palo and High Magic, all without formal training or supervision! Not only was the phrase "jack-of-all-trades and a master of none" applicable to her, as she knew virtually nothing about any of the aforementioned practices, her initial knowledge base of Hoodoo dwindled to complete gibberish when she spoke of it.

Being unfocused and confused during spiritual quests opens the doors for negative entities to attempt to trick or seduce people into following the wrong road. Jesus Christ pursued a vision quest fasting in the desert. In his weakened state, the Devil attempted to seduce him. Luckily, he remained focused and resisted all of Satan's temptations. Thus, the lesson to be learned is to remain focused.

If you are pursuing a particular spiritual path, here are a few tips to ensure mastery of your quest while remaining focused:

* When you receive appealing information regarding another path, keep that information and file it under future paths to be explored. There's always time to do so, once you have fully learned all you need to know to achieve mastery in your quest.

* If any information learned on your present path is either undesirable or inconsistent with your beliefs, seek clarity from your teacher. If further information is consistently unappealing, either seek a new teacher or leave the path completely.

* Most importantly, avoid temptation. If someone has something better to offer, remember that if it seems too good to be true, then it is!

Avoiding Negative Entities While Petitioning for Assistance

When petitioning for assistance or aid, always remember that each of us has a spiritual court we can call on for assistance in our lives and our spellwork. They are readily available to us, and they are much safer to petition as they are only looking out for our best interests. You simply must have faith in this as a fact. Just to name a few, you could summon:

* God Almighty, the Lord, the Divine
* The angels and archangels of Heaven

* Your Guardian Angel
* Figures from the Bible, according to their history and your need
* Catholic saints, according to their patronage
* The deities of your own religion or spiritual practice
* Your Spirit Guides
* Your ancestors who love you from time immemorial to those recently deceased—make that clear as there are ancestors who do not love you
* Decreased friends who understand your need and wish to help
* Deceased pets who loved you dearly and would do anything in their power to help

Formal prayers are a type of invocation, and they ought to be recited with thought, passion, and vision. Envision what you are reciting. If you are calling on a saint, envision the saint's presence. Feel that entity around you or in front of you. The content of the prayer also ought to be envisioned. Always remember that doubt is the precursor to desperation—which may draw unknown entities.

Actions to Take If Approached by an Entity

If there is an entity within our visual perception, it will often first appear as a see-through silhouette or a shadow that, more likely than not, slowly materializes into a more definite form wearing clothing. If the entity is benevolent, all that is needed is to alert them that you are frightened. On hundreds of occasions benevolent entities have appeared to me and gracefully disappeared after I have lovingly stated: "Your appearance is scaring me. Please go away. God Bless you and rest in peace." They will unassumingly fade away in the opposite of how they appeared: clothing first, then the silhouette will gradually dematerialize.

If the entity is a negative force, it will not leave when asked. If it attempts to make verbal contact with you—most likely audible within your left ear—do not answer it and do not attempt to reason with it. Whether silent or speaking, if it comes closer to you, do not panic.

Instead, with a spray bottle of Holy Water in hand (and I always keep a bottle in my refrigerator), take control of the situation as if chasing away mosquitoes with a can of insect repellent. Firmly spray it, multiple times, while demanding that it leave your home immediately. Tell the entity it was neither invited into your home nor is its presence wanted. Keep spraying and do so chasing it toward the door. Once the entity is near the door, open it and scream for it to "GET OUT!"

After its departure, slam the door behind it. Immediately spray the entire house with the Holy Water, then make lines at every doorway and all of your windowsills with sea salt. Later, make additional lines with either Holy Oil or Protection Oil. Then, pray Psalm 91 aloud for protection. Eventually, you must ponder and diagnose the circumstances that enticed it to make an approach and then correct those vulnerabilities.

Assaults by Sleep Demons

Hags

As previously discussed, these demonic witches or entities capable of shape-shifting, usually appearing as old ugly women, most often show up as nightmares. In Hoodoo, it is believed that they are capable of "hag-riding" by immobilizing their victims, while choking and cursing them.

If you are experiencing these sensations, first visit a licensed physician to ensure that this is not a medical condition known as sleep paralysis. This disorder occurs in cases of narcolepsy, low potassium, seizures, and other physiological dis-eases while causing body and speech immobilization accompanied with visual, auditory, or tactile hallucinations.

When and if sleep paralysis is ruled out, make all attempts to prevent these episodes by maintaining protection both on your person and in your bedroom. It is said that if they leave a wet spot, it is their skin that they will return to retrieve. Saturate the wet spot with salt to wither away their skin and ultimately destroy them.

Incubi and Succubi

If you are sexually assaulted by these demons, they will most likely return a second time. Rubbing Vicks Vaporub, a camphor-based ointment, on your body and especially between your legs—without touching your genitals, where it might cause irritation or be painful—will act as a repellent. The ointment may also be applied to the four corners of your bedsheets.

When All Else Fails

Just as bacteria may resist or become resistant to certain antibiotics, negative forces may resist the spiritual armor set up to repel them. When this occurs, it is usually because these forces have already anchored before you became aware of their presence, thus a task-oriented eradication ritual must be implemented. Ritual instructions will be provided in the next chapter.

8

The Thirteen-Day Eradication Ritual

With my technique, hundreds of clients have successfully rid themselves of forceful curses as well as unwanted spiritual entities that had been plaguing them using this intensive ritual.

However, if possessions, portals, or severe poltergeist activities—to be discussed in the next chapter—are present, I strongly advise to instead seek the help of an expert in these fields rather than attempting to resolve the issues alone. Experts have years of essential training and experience and are well-prepared for combat! Once they have exterminated the problem, you may then follow up with this ritual.

If you belong to a religion or spiritual group, first seek counsel and advice from your leader, as there might be specific rituals in your practice contradictory to this one. My ritual is Judeo-Christian based and therefore requires prayers and the symbolic objects of the same. Never practice any ritual or recite any prayers that contradict your core belief system.

Gather the Tools Needed

We've already explored most of these items in previous chapters, and, hopefully, when you review the list, they will arouse familiarity. A brief description will follow those items not previously discussed or requiring special emphasis.

To Spiritually Cleanse the Home

Pentagram of Solomon, cleansed and blessed, to wear as a necklace

Ammonia

Chinese Wash

Florida Water

A brand-new mop

A bucket

2 spray bottles

Thirteen Herbs for Thirteen-Day Bathing

This bath is designed to vigorously remove negativity, repair the aura, and provide protection. Prepared 13-Herb Baths may be purchased from most Hoodoo and Conjure stores as well as other spiritual shops.

If you wish to make your own formula, you may select from the list here, which provides more than thirteen options in the event of allergies. Choose only thirteen herbs from the list. It is strongly advisable to include the rue in your formula as it is the key ingredient for most uncrossing and protection prescriptions.

Although referred to as a 13-Herb formula, minerals may be used in place of an herb. For instance, my personal 13-Herb Bath contains kosher salt along with twelve herbs for a total of thirteen.

The herbs in the following list serve many functions; however, only their uncrossing, jinx-removing, and/or protection properties will be highlighted here. The herbs and minerals are referenced from the books *Hoodoo Herb and Root Magic: Materia of African-American Conjure* by catherine yronwode and *Cunningham's Encyclopedia of Magical Herbs* by Scott Cunningham. These books are highly recommended for a comprehensive study of the magical properties of herbs, roots, and minerals.

- ★ **Agrimony** (*Agrimonia eupatoria*): Wards off curses, provides protection.

- ★ **Angelica** (*Angelica archangelica*): Contains uncrossing properties.

- ★ **Bay leaves** (*Laurus nobilis*): Wards off evil.

- ★ **Boldo** (*Boldoa fragrans*): Wards off evil.

- ★ **Boneset** (*Eupatorium ageratoides*): Wards off jinxes.

- ★ **Burdock/bat weed** (*Arctium lappa*): Contains both uncrossing and protection properties.

- ★ **Caraway** (*Carum carvi*): Protection and healing.

- ★ **Celandine** (*Chelidonium*): Protection, especially against witches.

- ★ **Cinquefoil/five finger grass** (*Potentilla anserina*): Uncrossing and protection.

- ★ **Eucalyptus** (*Eucalyptus globulus, Eucalyptus spp.*): Eradicates evil and protects.

- ★ **Flaxseed** (*Linum usitatissimum*): Wards off evil.

- ★ **Hyssop** (*Hyssopus officinalis*): A purification herb.

- ★ **Lemongrass** (*Andropogon*): Wards off evil and brings in good luck.

- ★ **Peony** (*Paeonia*): Jinx breaker.

* **Rosemary** (*Rosemarinus officinalis*): Used for cleansing and purifying negativity.

* **Rue** (*Ruta graveolens*): Jinx breaker and protection.

* **Salt** (*sodium chloride*): My preference is kosher salt or sea salt, which is used for purification and protection.

The easiest preparation is to place thirteen tablespoons of every herb into a plastic bag or a jar and mix well. When you are ready to initiate the bath ritual by steeping the herbs, just use one tablespoon of the mixture per day. Also have on hand a small pot in order to steep the herbs and a small strainer.

Showering In-Between Rituals Baths

The 13-Herb Bath does not remove debris from the skin or other areas of the body. You may shower in-between your bathing rituals with Rue Soap. This is not a substitute for the 13-Herb Bath, but rather a complementary supplement.

Tibetan Purging Incense Powder

Although it is not my intention to showcase brand-name products, the Tibetan Purging Incense manufactured by Zambala, Inc. has brought great success for me as well as hundreds, if not thousands, of others. It is of supreme quality and both formulated and prepared under strict religious guidelines under the supervision of a religious master who is also the national-level incense maker of Tibet. Following its composition, the incense is then subsequently blessed for forty-nine consecutive days in a grand prayer ceremony, empowering it to remove spiritual impurities, conquer demonic activities, abolish obstacles, alleviate negative karma, provide protection, bring forth promising energies, and promote numerous other spiritual values.

While this incense is designed for the direct or self-lighting method—meaning that it is capable of burning on its own once ignited—my preference is to place it on a hot charcoal disc, then concurrently ignite the incense. This method ensures even combustion along with the ultimate distribution of incense smoke.

Some Tibetans disagree with my method, professing that the chemical composition of the charcoal will interfere with the spiritual properties of the incense, but my experience has not supported their statements. The final decision is solely up to the user to either incorporate the charcoal disc or to proceed exclusively with the direct method. Either way, the incense must be placed in a fireproof container. You will need:

A censer: A vessel designed to burn incense.

A long match or lighter: Ensure that these are longer to prevent burns upon ignition.

13 charcoal discs (optional)

Remaining Necessary Items

Camphor resin squares: Containing both purifying and protection properties.

Small glass cup: For placement of camphor and Florida Water.

Holy Bible: To set under the bed—can be purchased for one dollar.

Scissors: For placement over the Holy Bible.

St. Benedict medal(s): To position over main entranceways.

Holy Water: To spray on both yourself and around your dwelling.

Additional spray bottle: Container for the Holy Water.

Sea salt: To seal all entranceways such as windowsills and door entrances.

Blessing Oil: Bestows either holy or divine strength.

Holy Oil: To maintain a connection with God.

Protection Oil: With slight variations in label names, quality oils must contain the proper herbs and/or essential oils that provide protection.

Rue Oil: For protection and ridding oneself of negative energies.

2 uncrossing glass vigil candles: To maintain spiritual assistance. Two are needed for continuity during the thirteen-day ritual period.

A picture of yourself (with eyes showing): To set under the uncrossing candles.

Spiritually Cleanse Your Home First

Prior to performing the ritual, your home must first be cleansed. Depending on the size of the dwelling, it may take anywhere from a day to several days. Although the spiritual home cleansing is considered an independent task, the ritual must be initiated immediately following its completion.

Priority One

First and foremost, don your Pentagram of Solomon pendant. The chain ought to be long enough in order for the pentagram to lay over your sternum or breastbone. This is a priority because as the home is cleansed of negativity, those very particles may feverishly attempt to find refuge anywhere, including on your body, and the pentagram will prevent them from doing so.

The Intense Spiritual House Cleansing

Clutter is a sanctuary for negative forces and, therefore, must be removed. But prior to removing it, attempt to exterminate the particles within it by pouring Florida Water into one of the spray bottles and lightly spraying over the clutter. Afterward, it is safe to remove and reorganize the accumulated assemblage. Keep your spray bottle of Florida Water nearby.

Next, fill your bucket with water and add the appropriate amount of ammonia, according to packaging instructions. Harmful energies as entities are sensitive to ammonia. Wash any floor surfaces where using the chemical will not cause damage, such as bathroom floors, porcelain fixtures, and linoleum flooring. Do not allow ammonia to come into contact with vulnerable surfaces, such as wood floors and any furniture. When this task is completed, empty the content of the bucket into the toilet and flush. Thoroughly rinse your mop and bucket with warm water to eliminate the residual ammonia.

Now, each room must be cleansed individually and completely with the Chinese Wash prior to moving on to the next room. Refill your bucket with warm water and add one-quarter cup of the Chinese Wash to this, and then, agitate the mixture. Fill the other spray bottle with this mixture, as it will be used for carpets or unreachable areas.

As you work from room to room, start by washing the walls. Then, work downward and pay special attention to cleaning any windows, windowsills, doors, and thresholds. The last surface to clean is the floor—and you may mop over what has been previously washed with ammonia water—before going to the next room. Carpeting may be lightly sprayed with the mixture in your spray bottle or use it with a carpet shampooer.

Prior to leaving a room, open any door or window within that given room. Then, spray Florida Water into the air while reciting Psalm 84 aloud. This assists the flow of negative forces to the outside world rather than allowing them to flee into another room within the dwelling. Afterward, close the window or door to prevent the forces from reentering.

Before cleansing the next room, empty your bucket down the toilet and flush. Refill your bucket with warm water and one-quarter cup of Chinese Wash. Repeat the process until every room in the home has been spiritually cleansed.

Begin the Thirteen-Day Ritual

Day 1

Step 1. Uncrossing Vigil Candle

Once the entire home has been spiritually cleansed, select a location to set your candle, ensuring that it will sit atop a fireproof surface. Place your picture, with eyes showing, facing upward on this surface, then set the candle directly over your picture. Recite Psalm 29 aloud, which calls to God to drive away evil forces and restore peace.

Keep the candle consistently lit and pray over it once daily. The glass vigil candle will burn anywhere from five to seven days. Once the wax is totally consumed and the flame has extinguished itself, light the second candle and repeat the process. If both candles are totally consumed before the thirteen-day ritual has been completed, do not be concerned as the goal has already been fulfilled with the vigil candles. For the remaining days, simply light a two-inch tealight or votive candle on a daily basis while reciting the psalm. Remember to state your petition prior to closing the prayer with the word *Amen.*

PSALM 29

1 Give unto the Lord, O ye mighty, give unto the Lord glory and strength.

2 Give unto the Lord the glory due unto his name; worship the Lord in the beauty of holiness.

3 The voice of the Lord is upon the waters: the God of glory thundereth: the Lord is upon many waters.

4 The voice of the Lord is powerful; the voice of the Lord is full of majesty.

5 The voice of the Lord breaketh the cedars; yea, the Lord breaketh the cedars of Lebanon.

6 He maketh them also to skip like a calf; Lebanon and Sirion like a young unicorn.

7 The voice of the Lord divideth the flames of fire.

8 The voice of the Lord shaketh the wilderness; the Lord shaketh the wilderness of Kadesh.

9 The voice of the Lord maketh the hinds to calve, and discovereth the forests: and in his temple doth every one speak of his glory.

10 The Lord sitteth upon the flood; yea, the Lord sitteth King for ever.

11 The Lord will give strength unto his people; the Lord will bless his people with peace. Amen

Step 2. The Bathing Ritual

Your cleansings will be performed around the same time daily. In the Hoodoo tradition, it is believed that these baths ought to be performed in the early morning hours; however, these baths have been just as effective for my clients when performed at any time, as long as the timing is consistent.

Fill your bathtub with warm water or any temperature that is comfortable. Then, prepare your herbal mixture. Pray Psalm 23 over the herbs and ask God to bless and awaken them and ask for them to be used to remove negativity.

Boil three cups of water. When the water boils, add one tablespoon of the premixed herbal blend to the water. Immediately turn the heat off and allow the herbs to steep in the hot water for exactly thirteen minutes. After thirteen minutes have passed, take the pot and a strainer to the bathtub. Immediately strain the herbs while allowing the infused water to flow into the bathtub. Set the strained herbs aside.

Prior to entering the bathtub, ensure you have a bottle of Blessing Oil in the bathroom along with a copy of Psalm 37. Mine is laminated to prevent water damage.

Step into the bathtub and sit down. Begin to pray Psalm 37 aloud, which is a powerful uncrossing, jinx-removing, and spiritual restoration prayer. This psalm has forty verses, and the best approach is to recite the prayer and, in-between verses of your choice, immerse yourself completely in the water. Complete immersions must be performed a total of thirteen times.

The psalm is only to be recited once daily while performing the bathing ritual.

Try to remain in the bathtub for at least thirteen minutes. The time it takes to recite the psalm aloud while immersing oneself thirteen times is usually thirteen minutes or more.

Of all the psalms, this is my favorite. It describes humankind as we were in ancient times, which hasn't changed much to this day. Noteworthy is the fact that every time I perform an uncrossing for a client, a side effect of reciting this psalm is it brings me great luck!

PSALM 37

1 Fret not thyself because of evildoers, neither be thou envious against the workers of iniquity.

2 For they shall soon be cut down like the grass, and wither as the green herb.

3 Trust in the Lord, and do good; so shalt thou dwell in the land, and verily thou shalt be fed.

4 Delight thyself also in the Lord: and he shall give thee the desires of thine heart.

5 Commit thy way unto the Lord; trust also in him; and he shall bring it to pass.

6 And he shall bring forth thy righteousness as the light, and thy judgment as the noonday.

7 Rest in the Lord, and wait patiently for him: fret not thyself because of him who prospereth in his way, because of the man who bringeth wicked devices to pass.

8 Cease from anger, and forsake wrath: fret not thyself in any wise to do evil.

9 For evildoers shall be cut off: but those that wait upon the Lord, they shall inherit the earth.

10 For yet a little while, and the wicked shall not be: yea, thou shalt diligently consider his place, and it shall not be.

11 But the meek shall inherit the earth; and shall delight themselves in the abundance of peace.

12 The wicked plotteth against the just, and gnasheth upon him with his teeth.

13 The Lord shall laugh at him: for he seeth that his day is coming.

14 The wicked have drawn out the sword, and have bent their bow, to cast down the poor and needy, and to slay such as be of upright conversation.

15 Their sword shall enter into their own heart, and their bows shall be broken.

16 A little that a righteous man hath is better than the riches of many wicked.

17 For the arms of the wicked shall be broken: but the Lord upholdeth the righteous.

18 The Lord knoweth the days of the upright: and their inheritance shall be for ever.

19 They shall not be ashamed in the evil time: and in the days of famine they shall be satisfied.

20 But the wicked shall perish, and the enemies of the Lord shall be as the fat of lambs: they shall consume; into smoke shall they consume away.

21 The wicked borroweth, and payeth not again: but the righteous sheweth mercy, and giveth.

22 For such as be blessed of him shall inherit the earth; and they that be cursed of him shall be cut off.

23 The steps of a good man are ordered by the Lord: and he delighteth in his way.

24 Though he fall, he shall not be utterly cast down: for the Lord upholdeth him with his hand.

25 I have been young, and now am old; yet have I not seen the righteous forsaken, nor his seed begging bread.

26 He is ever merciful, and lendeth; and his seed is blessed.

27 Depart from evil and do good; and dwell for evermore.

28 For the Lord loveth judgment, and forsaketh not his saints; they are preserved for ever: but the seed of the wicked shall be cut off.

29 The righteous shall inherit the land, and dwell therein for ever.

30 The mouth of the righteous speaketh wisdom, and his tongue talketh of judgment.

31 The law of his God is in his heart; none of his steps shall slide.

32 The wicked watcheth the righteous, and seeketh to slay him.

33 The Lord will not leave him in his hand, nor condemn him when he is judged.

34 Wait on the Lord, and keep his way, and he shall exalt thee to inherit the land: when the wicked are cut off, thou shalt see it.

35 I have seen the wicked in great power, and spreading himself like a green bay tree.

36 Yet he passed away, and, lo, he was not: yea, I sought him, but he could not be found.

37 Mark the perfect man, and behold the upright: for the end of that man is peace.

38 But the transgressors shall be destroyed together: the end of the wicked shall be cut off.

39 But the salvation of the righteous is of the Lord: he is their strength in the time of trouble.

40 And the Lord shall help them, and deliver them: he shall deliver them from the wicked, and save them, because they trust in him. Amen

When finished bathing, step out of the tub and either blot yourself dry with a clean towel or air-dry. Immediately anoint the crown of you head and the back of your neck with Blessing Oil. Wear clean clothing. Discard the herbs outside with other foliage—symbolizing that they are returning from whence they came—in a respectful manner.

Step 3. Working Effectively with Purging Incense

Tibetan Purging Incense Powder behaves as a spiritual tear gas that repulses and suffocates negative forces. What do human beings do when exposed to tear gas? As an Air Force combat unit veteran, I can tell you that being exposed to it was one of the most horrific experiences I have ever endured. All of us did everything in our power to escape the toxic fumes. We will do the same in this step by enclosing the negative forces in a room, smoking them with the incense, and then providing them an escape route—away from the home!

After performing the ritual bath, donning your clean clothing, and respectfully discarding the herbs, you will now perform the incense ritual. Light a charcoal disc over your censer. When the charcoal gets good and hot, which you will know by its gray color, immediately close all of your doors and windows. Then place about one-half teaspoon of the incense into the concave portion of the charcoal disc. Keep additional incense on hand.

You will work one room at a time. Walk around the room with your censer, ensuring that the room is well-smoked with the incense. Then, immediately open one door or window and scream for the forces to leave your home immediately. Allow about one minute before closing the window or door behind them. Repeat this ritual in every room and add more incense to the censer if needed.

When the ritual is completed, set the censer on a fireproof surface and allow the incense to burn out completely. While waiting for the incense to cease burning, perform the following protection rituals. When the incense has been consumed, smolder the charcoal disc under running water to safeguard against any later sparking.

Step 4. Setting Up Protection with Salt and Oils

After performing the incense ritual, go outside with sea salt and Protection Oil. Throw the salt in the path before you to defend against any attempts at reentry by the banished forces. Then make barrier lines in front of your doors with the Protection Oil. It is believed that the forces cannot cross these barriers. Do this at any and all entrances into your home: garage, back door, side doors, etc.

Return inside your home. Make the sign of the cross on all of the closed windows and doors. Then, with either Rue Oil or Protection Oil, make additional protection barrier lines at all windowsills and around your windows and doorways. In other words, visualize any entity trying to enter your home and block those points.

Step 5. Sea Salt Water

Get a clear small drinking glass. Put some sea salt in your left hand. With your right index finger, make the sign of the cross over the sea salt and say: "In the Name of the Father, the Son, and the Holy Spirit, protect me." Put the salt into the glass. Put some water in the glass. Put the glass under your bed before you go to sleep. Every morning pour the salt water down the toilet to eliminate any impurities that may have collected. Clean the glass and repeat the process every night.

Step 6. The Backup Protection Enforcers

Open your Bible to Psalm 121. Hold the Bible in both hands and bend it outward to crack the spine and keep it open to that page. Open your scissors so that the blades are far apart and place it on top of the open pages of the Bible with the blades facing the top of the pages. Put this on the floor under your bed and keep it there permanently.

If you don't have a Bible, print or write out Psalm 121 and use it temporarily until you can purchase a Bible. This is only a temporarily substitution and does not replace the power of the Holy Bible.

PSALM 121

1 I will lift up mine eyes unto the hills, from whence cometh my help.

2 My help cometh from the Lord, which made heaven and earth.

*3 He will not suffer thy foot to be moved: he that keep-
eth thee will not slumber.*

*4 Behold, he that keepeth Israel shall neither slumber
nor sleep.*

*5 The Lord is thy keeper: the Lord is thy shade upon
thy right hand.*

*6 The sun shall not smite thee by day, nor the moon
by night.*

*7 The Lord shall preserve thee from all evil: he shall
preserve thy soul.*

*8 The Lord shall preserve thy going out and thy com-
ing in from this time forth, and even for evermore.*

Crumble one tablet of the camphor (there are usually four tablets in a block). Put it in a small glass cup, such as a votive candleholder or clear shot glass. Fill the rest of the cup with Florida Water. Keep this on the floor inside your house behind your front door. Refill as needed.

Hang the cleansed and blessed St. Benedict medal inside the house over your front door. My house has one hanging over every single door and window.

Spray your home, as well as yourself, as often as possible with Holy Water. You may also spray all living beings who share the home with you, and this includes your pets.

Days 2–13

Steps 1–5 will be repeated daily for a total of thirteen days. As noted earlier, step 1 only requires daily prayer over the lit candle until a new candle is needed.

Be consistent in your daily ritual routine. Many people ask what they ought to do if they accidentally skip a day. My answer is always the same: plan ahead! If a day is missed, the ritual has to be started again from the beginning. It's the same as having an infection and taking antibiotics to kill the bacteria: if you miss a day of the medication, it's an opportunity for the bacteria to become resistance to the drugs.

Missing a day of ritual performance is making a loud and clear statement of a lack of commitment, which negative forces view as a sign of weakness. You *must* demonstrate that you have the upper hand and will not, under any circumstances, tolerate their presence. Otherwise, they will persistently test you.

The other piece of advice I give all of my clients is to never tell anybody what you are doing or what you have done. If the negative forces were aimed at you on purpose, such as with a curse, then you've given the enemy valuable information. This advice applies to all spiritual work. Silence is golden!

After the Ritual

Upon completing this challenging ritual, about 99 percent of my clients report feeling refreshed and rejuvenated. One client even accused me of saving her marriage! But please remember that if you allow the same chaotic events to repeat themselves, you will be in the same situation as before. So ensure that your protection tools and techniques are up to par!

* Bathe often with Rue Soap to provide spiritual cleansing and protection.
* Apply Blessing Oil to yourself as often as possible.

* Replenish the sea salt water under your bed on a daily basis.

* Keep the camphor and Florida Water mixture maintained at the front door.

* The Bible and scissors are to remain under the bed.

* Frequently spray with Holy Water.

* Avoid collecting clutter.

* Cleanse and bless your medals at least two to three times a year.

* It is permissible to take one 13-Herb Bath anytime it is needed.

Remove Lingering Obstacles

After you finish performing the thirteen-day ritual, some blockages created by the negative forces may still linger. This does not mean that these forces are still at play, but it's more like they left in a hurry without first fixing what they broke. Think of it as a business card that was left behind. Such problems can be easily resolved with a Blockbuster Spell followed by a Road Opener Spell.

The question I most frequently hear regarding these spells is "What's the difference?" Imagine there is a brick wall and on the other side of that wall are many roads without street signs. The Blockbuster Spell will symbolically tear down the wall, while the Road Opener Spell provides street signs accompanied by guidance down the correct streets. That's the difference.

Blockbuster Spells

The two suggested Blockbuster Spells here are both equally effective. Start the ritual on a Monday. Some practitioners hold that this spell ought to be performed during a waning moon phase because that is a time to banish negativity, while others maintain that it ought to be performed during a waxing moon phase because this period brings in new opportunities. The choice is yours, but if you are performing a Road Opener Spell immediately afterward, try to coordinate the timing in order for the Road Opener Spell to be initiated during the waxing moon phase.

Blockbuster Spell 1

Purchase a Blockbuster glass-encased vigil candle. Starting on a Monday, place a picture of yourself with your eyes showing faceup on a fireproof surface, and then place the candle directly on the picture. Recite the Lord's Prayer, followed by Psalm 23, and, finally, the Road-Opening Prayer aloud every day. After each prayer, prior to saying *Amen* state your petition and ensure that it remains consistent each day. Do not change your requests.

The request may echo something like: "Please remove all obstacles that are preventing me from obtaining a job." Another example could be: "Please remove all blockages that are preventing me from obtaining a lover."

Do not ask to remove blockages to create an action of another person unless you clearly specify that there will be no harm to anyone. For instance, if you wanted to remove blockages preventing the return of a lover, not wording this the right way might cause someone physical injury in the process. So be prudent.

Blockbuster Spell 2

Obtain a nine-inch orange candle and cleanse it with salt water or Florida Water. Using a pencil, inscribe on it nine times in script from top to bottom with "Remove Obstacles." Do not lift your pencil when incising your petition in the wax.

Note that the direction of your inscription is opposite that directed in the Road Opener Spell. This is because, when we wish to bring something to us, we inscribe from bottom to top; when we wish for something or someone to go away, the inscription is top to bottom.

Anoint the candle with either Blockbuster Oil or olive oil. Immediately roll it in Blockbuster Incense or in a mixture of dried, crushed Blockbuster Herbs, which can be purchased from numerous spiritual shops.

Place a picture of yourself with your eyes showing faceup inside a glass candleholder. Then place the candleholder on a fireproof surface. Set the candle directly on the picture. Follow the instructions given in Blockbuster Spell 1. Despite what the product websites state, nine-inch candles burn for a period of 28–32 hours.

When the candle has extinguished itself, bury the candle wax and your picture either in your front yard or in a potted houseplant. If neither are an option, bury it near a consenting tree and ask that as the tree grows, so will your opportunities. Thank the tree, then pay it for its services with a dime and fresh water to drink.

On the next Monday that falls during the waxing moon phase, perform a Road Opener Spell. These spells can be found in chapter 6.

Calling on Good Spirits

Recently, a question posted on the internet piqued my interest: "If you clean the house of spirits, how do you get the good ones to come back?" The following are the two most common practices employed in the spiritual practices to ensure that we maintain a connection with the good spirits.

Burning Sweetgrass

A Cherokee shaman once taught me that burning sweetgrass (*Hierochloe odorata*) is very attractive to good spirits. He elaborated that after smudging with white sage for purification, immediately follow this ritual by burning sweetgrass. In other words, get rid of the bad, then bring in the good. Sweetgrass is most commonly sold in a dried, braided form. When burned, its odor is sweet and appealing.

Ancestral Altar—Beginners, Keep It Simple!

Many spiritual practitioners actively engage in ancestral veneration as a means to maintain contact and spiritual assistance with our relatives who have passed on. This has gone on around the world for centuries, and as time passes and archeologists develop technological means to discover and further study our ancient past, they are learning that ancestral veneration was practiced even before recorded ancient history.

Ancestral altars can be created to serve as an area where the ancestors take ownership and a point of human-to-ancestor contact. In other words, it is their home and a location where we can visit and converse.

Depending on the religion or spiritual path, altars vary from bare-minimum basics to elaborate, ornate extravagances. For the beginner, all that is needed are a few basic items, while keeping in mind that your ancestors will greatly appreciate the thought and effort.

A basic, simple, and effective altar for beginners would include:

* Small table
* White cotton cloth
* White votive or glass-encased vigil candle
* Glass of fresh cold water
* Fresh white flowers (carnations are inexpensive and live longer)
* A religious object representing your ancestor's faith

Determine a site to designate as a permanent location for the altar. Set the table in that area, then cover it with the white cloth. Position the religious object in the center of the table opposite the side where you stand, then set the candle in front of it. Place the flowers and the glass of fresh water on the altar.

Recite a prayer aloud that has meaning for both you and your religious or spiritual tradition. Then, announce your birth name and your dedication of the altar. It is suggested not to specifically or individually name unknown ancestors, as you don't know which ones did not get along in life and you don't want any animosity to continue in your home.

This is my preferred verbiage: "This altar is dedicated to God, all the archangels, all the saints, my Spirit Guides, Guardian Angels, and ancestors. Treat this altar as if it is your home. Enjoy your candle and fresh water." Do not ask for any favors for a few weeks. Instead, engage in casual conversations with them without unloading your problems and offer fresh water daily.

As time passes, you will feel the need to add more objects to your altar. If you experience unusual odors such as coffee, food, cigarette smoke, etc., it is an ancestor asking for this to be placed on the altar. It is also a great sign of their established residency!

9

Severe Spiritual Activities Requiring Professional Help

In keeping with my proclamation that "knowledge is power," this chapter is solely to provide information regarding severe negative spiritual activities and how to seek the proper help to address them. After you have read this section, you will hopefully be able to identify and understand what might be occurring.

Occasionally, people may come across negative forces that are highly sophisticated—even ancient—that have accrued a knowledge and skill-base the ordinary person lacks in order to survive. When these types of entities or events are encountered, the average person cannot diagnose, control, or eradicate them because they lack the excruciating amount of training and experience to do so.

Furthermore, being a witch or practitioner does not necessarily mean that such an individual has expertise in all areas relating to spirituality because it's impossible to accrue all that in one lifetime. There are countless disciplines for which it would take ages to study and absorb the knowledge necessary to gain proficiency in their varying fields. This is the reason that certain practitioners develop expertise in only a single discipline.

If someone were to get a small laceration on their hand, that person would readily go to their local family doctor to get stitches. But what if the hand had been completely severed at the wrist? That family doctor lacks the knowledge base to reconnect it. Instead, the doctor would seek a hand surgeon to take immediate control of the patient's case because that surgeon had spent years studying, experiencing, and gaining expertise in both domains of orthopedics and specialized surgery.

Earlier in this book, we looked at John Zaffis's insights on possessed objects. He is an expert in dealing with possessions because he is a demonologist as well as a paranormal researcher and investigator. His example demonstrates expertise in a subspecialty of spirituality that took excruciating years to conquer. Therefore, as we explore the more difficult scenarios, keep in mind that specialized experts must be sought out in order to achieve resolution in these cases.

Hauntings

A haunting is a paranormal phenomenon in which a spiritual entity, such as a ghost, spirit, or supernatural being, makes habitual appearances in a given location. According to PsychicLibrary.com, there are four common types of hauntings: residual, intelligent, poltergeist, and demonic.

Residual hauntings: The most common type of haunting is the residual haunting where there is no communication or attempted communication between an entity and human. Instead, the events witnessed—such as hearing sounds, seeing the same apparition in the same place, or witnessing an event repetitiously—are simply records of energies imprinted or absorbed in the area where the event took place. The result is similar to watching a movie over and over again.

Intelligent hauntings: These are what we consider a classic haunting. It is when a human is able to interact and/or communicate with the entity. Although it may be a deceased loved one visiting and attempting to communicate, be aware of the possibility that a negative entity might be disguising its voice in order to trick a person into believing it is someone else.

Poltergeist hauntings: Poltergeist means "noisy ghost" in German. These entities, either playful or harmful, might make disturbing noises and/or use objects that can be thrown, moved, or hidden. Sometimes, objects will disappear and reappear. Often, but not always, these types of hauntings are associated with adolescent females living in the home.

Demonic hauntings: As discussed in earlier chapters, the goal of the demon is to gain control over a person, as a parasite uses its host. It will attempt to deceive or trick an individual. It can enter and act benevolent for a while until it gains the upper hand. If you believe that you have seen a figure that resembles a human but then you think it's an animal, it might be demonic since they are capable of shape-shifting. Demonic entities can also appear as dark shadows.

Actions to Take If You Suspect a Haunting

If there are subtle poltergeist activities, first ensure that a wild animal or human is not the culprit. A friend of mine once urgently summoned me to her home because she was hearing unusual noises, while many objects originally showcased on her shelves were either broken or on the floor. The "supernatural being" in this case was simply a squirrel that had accidentally entered the home and was frantically attempting to find its way back outside. But that squirrel did indeed make some intimidating noises!

Most importantly, if there is excessive disorder or rearrangement of your belongings, call the police immediately. Even if you suspect a poltergeist, never dismiss the possibility that it could be a human intruder. Never be embarrassed to contact the police. Your safety must be your highest priority.

If the poltergeist activity threatens the safety of any person or pet, leave the home immediately. This also applies to any suspicions of a demonic haunting.

Do not contact the first available person who claims to be a spiritual practitioner. A woman once frantically reached out to a pseudo-practitioner she came across in a rushed internet search because a couch pillow had flown at her from across the room while she was home alone. Then more flying pillows subsequently followed.

This pseudo-practitioner insisted that his visitation charge was $1,000. Panic-stricken and desperate, she agreed to his fee. He promptly arrived, empty-handed, walked around her apartment but did nothing, and insisted that she remove her clothing and lie in the bathtub within his view. When she exited the tub and donned her clothing, he collected his money, handed her a mojo bag (a small flannel bag containing magical items), and left.

I'm not quite sure how removing one's clothing, taking a bath, and owning a mojo bag could interrupt poltergeist activity, but this was clearly fraudulent activity. Additionally, the sexual undertones of being naked in his sight were disturbing. He was reported to the proper channels but sadly is still presenting himself as a spiritual practitioner.

If you suspect a haunting, the proper action to take is to contact a legitimate paranormal investigation team. They have the proper training, experience, knowledge, and equipment to make a correct diagnosis.

How to Find a Legitimate Paranormal Investigation Team

I asked my friend, Russell Azbill, a noted paranormal investigator of fifteen years, how to identify a good team versus a bad one. Investigator Azbill states: "From the start, the person seeking help must interview the team to determine the following:

* ★ How long have the team members been paranormal investigators?

* ★ What are the individual team members' backgrounds?

* ★ Do they know the basics of paranormal investigations?

* ★ Does the team possess at least the basic amount of equipment to properly perform a paranormal investigation?

* ★ Do they understand and acknowledge their personal limitations?

* ★ Do they have big egos and sensationalize the work that they do? They should not.

* ★ Have any of the team members, especially the leader, had any past integrity issues or been convicted of a crime?

* ★ Have they ever gone to a location and found nothing? The answer should be yes.

* Do they respect the spirits or not?

* Do they provoke the spirits? The answer should be no.

* Do they have multiple references they can provide? Due to privacy issues, the team may not be able to provide references, but you should always ask anyway.

* Have any of the paranormal team members had a personal encounter with a spirit prior to becoming an investigator?

* Do they have the resources to eradicate any spiritual intrusions?"

Azbill concludes by commenting that it is best to interview the team leader in person and look for signs of deception. His advice is to interview at least two to three different teams in order to make a comparative analysis and, ultimately, a decision.

Azbill agrees that big egos and sensationalizing the work are not an attribute. Sadly, I have met a few whose egos were so inflated that they were focused on self-promotion rather than a genuine interest in their clients' well-being. Take notice of their focus for your own safety and emotional well-being. If they show a lack of concern, then it's not the right team for you.

Finally, consider that simply confirming a genuine haunting is not enough to achieve a final solution. Ask the team what will happen if it is determined to be a demonic haunting. Are demonologists or exorcists readily accessible to them? What can be done to eradicate a poltergeist or other type of haunting? Is there a person available with the skills to eradicate the problematic spiritual entities and how soon can this person be available? In other words, ensure that they have the means to resolve the haunting.

Interdimensional Portals

Interdimensional portals—from here on in referred to as portals—sometimes also called star gates or vortexes, are entrances, doorways, or gates allowing passage between other worlds or dimensions and ours. Knowledge of such portals has been documented in ancient texts from all around the world, while recent ongoing reported and documented cases of their existence continue.

Their locations vary and could be virtually anywhere, including within large buildings or bodies of water. Upon encountering a portal, people have reported unusual temperature changes, the feeling of enhanced energies, and colors being extraordinarily vibrant.

Entities encountered via portals may be benevolent, neutral, or malevolent in nature. Various ones are capable of shape-shifting—however, not all are demonic in nature—and may take the form of an animal, such as an owl, in order to unassumingly survey and monitor this world without being noticed. However, Nigel Mortimer, an expert on the subject of portals, states in his book *UFOs, Portals and Gateways* that the entities appear in various forms. He says that some have been described as looking like us, some look different, and "some are likened to something from the farthest reaches of the imagination." Among the countless variations are:

* Blue-skinned entities
* Flying rods
* Giant beings
* Shadow entities
* Giant wolves
* Black dogs

* Spirits, ghosts

* Extraterrestrial entities (grays, reptilians, etc.)

The most common phenomena reported to me are mists that seem to have their own intelligence and countless balls of light of varying colors. People living near a portal may also experience poltergeist activities.

Actions to Take If You Suspect a Portal Is Nearby

Do not attempt physical or verbal contact with the portal and/or any entities. If an entity attempts contact with you, ignore it, as you don't know its intentions. Most importantly, walk away from the portal and stay away from it. Immediately call in the experts such as:

* **Paranormal investigative teams:** They can provide diagnosis as well as attempt a resolution.

* **Mutual UFO Network (MUFON):** A field investigator will be assigned to your case. Numerous FIs are also paranormal investigators.

* **Native American reservations:** Many Native American shamans have expertise in this arena.

Spirit Attachments

Sometimes harmless entities or earthbound ghosts will attempt to attach themselves to us for various reasons such as experiencing confusion or loneliness, being attracted to a person, feeling familiarity with a person, and other intentions. If the aura is healthy, they cannot anchor to it and therefore can be easily detached. Sometimes detachment is as simple as wiping the crown of your head with your hand, then shaking the hand to rid yourself of it. Other times just a crystal cleansing, a spritz from a spray bottle filled with any of the recommended spiritual waters on the crown of the head and/or the rest of the chakras, spiritual baths, etc., will chase it away.

However, there are times when spiritual attachments can be difficult to remove. Throughout this book, we have explored numerous scenarios that may cause emotional and spiritual imbalances, and we know that being in prolonged states of despair can lead to the suppression of or damage to the aura. When the aura is impaired, it becomes susceptible to further harm, especially if there are existing tears or holes. These are ideal conditions for an entity to anchor itself into all of the energy fields: aura and chakras. They do so by attaching cords to these primary areas. Later, the host is depleted of energy because the entities are consuming it for their own strength and survival.

In some cases, attachments occur when inexperienced novices open a floodgate of entities during their psychic quests. This happens because the novice lacks the knowledge to understand the consequences of their actions, doesn't have proper protection techniques in place, and also lacks supervision. Sadly, in other cases, entities will have been blatantly invited to attach themselves by, and to, the host.

The attached entities are not necessarily malevolent. They could be just lost lonely souls who have found comfort with their host and won't risk the chance of losing that sense of security. Others are indeed of a wicked nature.

As a German Shepherd dog owner for more than fifty years, I think these contrasting scenarios are comparable to flea or tick infestations. Although a flea can be harmful, it will ride on its dog and feed on this host's blood for nourishment. But fleas can be easily removed with the application of a flea spray or bath, just as a harmless attachment can be easily eliminated with spiritual sprays or cleansings. On the other hand, ticks will grasp the skin, cut holes into it, then burrow deep inside. When they remain with the host for prolonged periods of time, they engorge themselves with the host's blood and, more often than not, will deliver, in return, serious and/or fatal diseases. The deeper the tick has burrowed, the more difficult it is to remove. Thus experience and expertise are needed to do so. When the tick is removed, it will leave waste products behind.

The initial signs and symptoms for both flea and tick infestations are virtually identical, and the first action to take is to immediately attempt to resolve the issue with sprays and baths. If the problem persists, it is obviously a more complex matter, as with a burrowing tick; therefore, professional help is to be sought. The same principles and actions to take apply to spirit attachments. First, attempt to eradicate the entity with the techniques discussed in this book.

Additionally, you could be feeling a residual attachment for an entity leaving something behind in the energy field—as the tick leaves waste products in the dog's skin. This residual attachment is easier removed than an active attachment. If the problem persists, it is more likely there are active cords attached to the energy fields.

Some of the signs and symptoms associated with cord attachments include:

* Sleep disturbances and/or nightmares
* Intrusive thoughts
* Feeling as if someone is watching you or is in the room with you
* Hearing voices
* Suddenly possessing a new talent without training or experience
* Impetuous or impulsive behaviors
* General behavioral changes

* Insatiable hunger or loss of appetite
* Fatigue
* Suicidal ideations without reason
* A sudden preference toward isolation rather than socialization
* Unexplained sadness or anger

Please note that not all of these signs and symptoms must be present for there to be an attachment. However, the most obvious signs, such as changes in behaviors and thoughts, without reason or justification strongly indicate that there is another spirit hanging around. Those signs, accompanied with the feeling that someone is watching you, can confirm the diagnosis.

Actions to Take for Spiritual Attachments

First and foremost, make the decision that you will regain control of your life. I advise my clients to affirm aloud, numerous times daily: "This is *my* life, and nobody will share my body and my energies. These were gifted to me by God. They are all mine!"

Immediately begin seeking an expert in this field and initiate spiritual cleansing baths. Perform the baths daily, without a preset time limit, until the expert declares that the entity has been eradicated and you have confirmed this through your own feelings of its departure.

Find an expert in this field who is willing and capable of performing hands-on eradication. This may be a coven of witches who can identify and cut the cords or a therapist who specializes in cord detachments. Whomever you seek for assistance, ensure that they have expertise in this area. Mere website advertisements lacking substantial credentials weaken their credibility. Take the time and effort to research each individual you are considering.

Spirit Possessions

Due to the media sensationalizing walking corpses, most of the world is solely familiar with the concept of zombies, which are said to be involuntary reanimations of a human corpse. In reality, there are several classifications of spirit possession, and they can be of an involuntary or voluntary nature. In numerous cultures, it is believed that gods, demigods, saints, ancestors, spirits, Spirit Guides, Guardian Angels, ghosts, djinn, demons, and other spiritual entities are capable of possessing a human body. According to Wikipedia, "in a 1969 study funded by the National Institute of Mental Health, spirit possession beliefs were found to exist in 74 percent of a sample of 488 societies in all parts of the world."

When a possession is voluntary, it is usually the result of a summoning ritual performed by holy people and/or those exclusive or elite ones who have been selected and trained to do so. However, voluntary possessions do not always take place through ritual. Sometimes, the entity may have asked for and been granted permission. In any case, it is popularly believed that possession by benevolent entities will provide favorable effects to either the human host or those around them. Possession of an involuntary nature usually accomplished by demons, ill-willed ghosts, and other malevolent entities may produce damaging effects in the host. Yet even voluntary possessions, if uncontrolled, can be damaging if a negative entity is summoned. Let's explore a couple examples of both helpful and harmful possessions.

Helpful Possessions

Orishas

The religion of Santería venerates orishas. These are spirits who are as highly revered as gods/goddesses or saints.

This religion encompasses a hierarchical structure ranging from people who worship the orishas to those wishing to establish an intimate relationship with them. Those who seek a closer relationship will undergo an initiation rite to become either a *santero* (male) or *santera* (female). This rite establishes a union between a particular orisha and their "child."

If desired, the santero/a will later undertake a different rite to become fully capable of being what is lovingly referred to as the orisha's *caballo* ("horse" in Spanish because the orisha "mounts" their host) and then make themselves available for ceremonies.

When that particular orisha's presence is needed, the entity will be summoned through a drumming ceremony. The orisha then places the mind of the caballo in an unconscious, or dormant, state and takes control of the body. Next, the orisha attempts to help as many people as possible.

Orishas cannot occupy human bodies for prolonged periods of time because the body of the caballo cannot contain the immense amount of energy held within the orisha.

Ibbur

In Jewish folklore, this is a benevolent entity who possesses a person for positive intentions. Possession happens when a righteous spirit occupies a living person's body for a short period of time by joining or spiritually "impregnating" the existing soul to perform a just deed or to reveal a vital teaching.

Rabbi Geoffrey W. Dennis, author of *The Encyclopedia of Jewish Myth, Magic and Mysticism,* graciously granted me the honor of an exclusive interview regarding the two most popular types of possessions in Jewish folklore. This was a highly educational, as well as enthralling, conversation. Rabbi Dennis explained:

> There's a notion in the Bible that because the human body is spiritually permeable (God breathes life into lifeless clay), spirits are capable of transmigrating in and out of the human, as there are numerous reports of people being possessed by various pneumatic entities: the "spirit of wisdom," "The spirit of God," and "the spirit of prophecy." There is also at least one case of an "evil spirit" either possessing or haunting King Saul. This possible transmigration is described in the experiences of King Saul in the First Book of Samuel of The Bible. Thus, these biblical sources provide a justification for how a possession is possible.

> When an ibbur possesses a living body, or host, the person may or may not know it. In many circumstances, a spiritual person will actively seek the experience of the possession for a righteous purpose such as a revelation, a warning to a community, etc.

Harmful Possessions

Dybbuk

Rabbi Dennis continued to say:

> In contrast, a dybbuk (meaning "to cling" or "clinging spirit"), is the soul or spirit of a person who is unable to make a successful transition after death into the next realm and craves to be embodied again. They will then attempt a possession, because a soul disembodied is a tormented soul.

> Dybbuks are of an evil nature, but it is a byproduct of their transgressions in life, rather than coming from an infernal source. For instance, it is believed by many that the souls of the evil generation prior to the "Great

Flood" of the Bible are still around, unable to make that transition to a progressive realm.

Why certain people are vulnerable to being possessed is unclear, but it is perceived that dybbuks are able to enter the morally weak or ill. Signs to look for in confirming a possession are changes in behaviors, seizures, speaking in another language, etc.

Various aspects of a Jewish exorcism rite are similar to a Christian rite but different in others. There are some Christian exorcisms that involve physical force, but we do not engage in that practice.

The exorcism rite in Judaism is not fixed, as it is in Roman Catholicism, nor is there a standard for who may conduct an exorcism, but the rite usually begins by obtaining an interview to acquire their name, history, and to address the reasoning for their inability to move on. Sometimes, the dybbuk can be deceptive and/ or resistant, so it's important to be aware of inconsistencies in their answers.

Exorcism in Judaism is a surprisingly public event, with a minimum of ten men present to represent the community. As often, there will be many looking on, both family and neighbors.

Psalm 91 and Psalm 121 are often recited along with other Bible verses. A shofar or other ritual objects can be used, and the burning of sulfur is also a common practice. The goal of the exorcism is to rid the victim of the dybbuk, but to also help the dybbuk by providing guidance and absolution in order for it to make the transition. The exorcist will stay and remain talking to the dybbuk until it leaves.

We then look for signs that the dybbuk has left. Such signs may include passing gas or a bleeding spot on the body, which indicates that it has departed.

Cases of dybbuk possessions are still reported today, but the incidents are rare. There is far less evidence for the notion of demonic possession in Judaism. Aside from the incidents reported in the Gospels, canonical Jewish sources only consider evil spirits as a source of illness, and it is not clear whether Jews in antiquity thought that the illness-inflicting imps actually entered the body or simply haunted/attacked a person to inflict sickness.

We have a window into this belief from late antiquity, when some Jews, in common with their non-Jewish neighbors, would bury an "incantation bowl" or "demon bowl" under their doorstep to protect themselves from illness-bearing evil spirits.

Such bowls as have been found are filled with incantations against specific illnesses, the names of types of malevolent demons and djinn, biblical verses, and, sometimes, a drawing of a malevolent spirit at the center of the bowl, illustrated as trapped in a magic circle or in fetters. It is believed that the Jews who used these regarded the bowls as a kind of spirit "mouse trap" that would catch the entities.

Demonic Possessions

A demonic possession occurs when a living person is inhabited and controlled by a demonic entity. Once they have taken up residence in the human body, they seek to destroy that person as well as anybody or anything associated with him/her. As had been previously emphasized in several chapters, these entities prey on those with unhealthy auras and seek an invitation. However, a formal request is not their only definition of an invitation; they see any lack of resistance to their presence and/or antics as approval.

Demonic entities seek what is known as "the weakest link" because it is easier to trick and deceive these people into compliancy and/or because they lack the knowledge or strength to resist their approaches. This includes children or those suffering from ailments such as alcoholism, anxiety, depression, drug addictions, illnesses, loneliness, and stress. Additionally, those recovering from having been in a comatose state or a near-death experience seem to often attract these entities.

Additional hazardous activities that also arouse their attention include:

* ★ Answering voices calling your name.
* ★ Attending demonic ceremonies.
* ★ Calling on unknown entities.
* ★ Moving into a dwelling that is already occupied by demonic entities.
* ★ Opening windows or doors after hearing knocking or tapping.
* ★ Unsupervised dabbling with the occult or spirits.

The Three Stages of Demonic Possession

Paranormal researchers generally agree that there are three stages of demonic possession. Although these stages are largely sequential and cumulative, there may be overlaps in the signs and symptoms of each. It is more important to be alert to the signals and behaviors rather than the stages.

Stage 1. Infestation: The Target Is Hunted by the Entity.

This is the stage when the entities seek approval to remain with the target. Therefore, it is crucial to immediately call for professional help to diagnose the causes of the following signs, especially if two or more are present:

* Animals dying.

* Children or pets suddenly developing an aversion to areas within the home.

* Children suddenly conversing with unseen forces (this is viewed as an invitation).

* Feeling or seeing a presence around you.

* Hearing voices, especially if in the left ear. Sometimes the voices appear friendly.

* Nightmares.

* Paranormal activity.

* Premonitions, told by the voices, are realized.

Stage 2. Oppression: The Entity Attaches Itself to the Target.

Along with signs of identical to spiritual cord attachment, other indicators that it is indeed a demonic possession usually include:

* Burning sensations on various areas of the body.

* Insatiable and sudden desire for the consumption of alcohol and/or drugs.

* Seeing unusual or unearthly looking creatures or dark shadows.

* Seizures.

* Voices provoking anger toward others or self-mutilation.

Stage 3. Possession: The Target Is Now Overtaken by the Demonic Entity.

The demonic entity is now in control most of the time of both the personality and the body. Its goal is solely to destroy the host and/or those around the host. The demonic entity will eventually convince the person to commit suicide, in hopes that their soul will be condemned to Hell forever. In this stage, the behaviors, signs, and symptoms are:

* Aversion to religious prayers, religious objects such as a crucifix, and Holy Water

* Blackouts

* Changes in physiological appearance

* Different voices coming out of the same person

* Excessive use of profanity

* Hatred of God, biblical, or other holy figures

* Obsession with killing animals

* Raging anger and violence

* Supernatural knowledge of people or of forthcoming events

Possession versus Emotional Instability or a Pretender

In an article published by Catholic News Agency, Father Cipriano de Meo, a Catholic priest who has been an exorcist since 1952, was interviewed on the topic of demonic possessions. When asked how to recognize the difference between an actual possession versus other causes for inappropriate behaviors, he answered: "This is a priority assessment as well as a vital part of the ministry of exorcism—not all cases of possessions are going to look the same, which is why it is so important for exorcists to go through rigorous training."

In my past research, it appears that legitimate exorcists in all religions and spiritual practices perform similar assessments prior to conducting an exorcism. Additionally, they are highly trained and experienced practitioners who are also well-versed in the psychological dynamics of the human psyche.

The Exorcist

The cases of documented possessions are on the rise along with the number of exorcisms being performed. Prior to his death, Father Gabriele Amorth, world-renowned priest, exorcist, and founder of International Association of Exorcists (AIE), claimed that he and his team had performed 160,000 exorcisms in the year 2013 alone.

There are only differing opinions and speculation as to why the number of possessions is rising, but as the number of cases increase so do the field of fraudulent exorcists who are ready, willing, and able to take advantage of these life-threatening situations to acquire fast and easy money. This is the reason that everyone must be very careful and thorough about whom one contacts for help.

First and foremost, *never* attempt to perform an exorcism! This rite is extremely dangerous and at times life-threatening. Sadly, these rites and rituals are easily accessible and can be found on the internet. But those words and actions mean absolutely nothing without rigorous training and experience. If you needed open heart surgery and the manual was accessible on the internet, would you allow a layman friend to perform that surgery on you? I hope not! In my humble opinion, an exorcism can be as serious as surgery.

If the afflicted is a member of a religious or spiritual practice, immediately contact the leader. This may be a priest or pastor of a church or a rabbi. Exorcisms are also performed by the experienced leaders of Hinduism, Taoism, Buddhism, and other religions and spiritual traditions. Sometimes, a Christian church leader is not readily available and will assign a highly trained professional under the leader's tutelage to perform a rite similar to an exorcism but is instead called a deliverance. There are also demonologists who perform these rites as well as paranormal investigators who have undergone the rigorous training to perform either an exorcism or a deliverance. But no matter whom you call, ensure that the person can provide references and prove their expertise in this specialty.

Having attended and assisted with three exorcisms in the distant past, it is my profound proclamation that exorcists are a breed of human beings that possess both nerves of steel and the patience of saints. They are courageous individuals with an overpowering sense of faith and compassion.

Who in their right mind would willingly enter a proverbial battlefield knowing full well that there is a strong chance of being insulted, humiliated, demoralized, and, worse yet, physically attacked all because they are helping someone? Who would enter this battlefield not knowing if they must endure this abuse for unknown amounts of time? Only an exorcist! In my personal opinion, these people were chosen by a higher authority to do such "dirty deeds" prior to even being born. No matter the exorcist's faith, religious or spiritual beliefs, or gender, each and every one of them have my undying respect.

My Experiences with Demonic Exorcism Rites

Nowadays, people are offering "remote exorcisms," meaning those accomplished from a distance. Although I am neither familiar with the rationale nor the mechanics of this concept, how it could be performed successfully is absolutely baffling to me. Rabbi Dennis briefly discussed the mechanics of exorcising a dybbuk, which is obviously a tedious and task-oriented job. By additionally relaying my own experiences, I hope it will provide insight as to what an exorcism entails as well as what both the victim and the exorcist and any assistant(s) endure. Afterward, feel free to examine what a remote exorcism entails to make your own comparative analysis and decisions.

Prior to performing the rite, the exorcist always insisted on an evaluation of the victim by a psychiatrist, which is an MD or DO who has thereafter completed a residency in psychiatry. He insisted on psychiatric evaluations in order to obtain both a physiological as well as a psychological profile simultaneously.

After consulting with the psychiatrist, and obviously with proper consent, the exorcist would then visit the home to perform his own assessment before arranging the rite. In this way, he could be properly prepared.

The first case I observed initially seemed relatively harmless. In fact, my first suspicions were that the victim was pretending, but I was wrong. It was a middle-aged woman, quiet, appearing to be demure in nature; however, looking back at the scenario, it was actually her spirit giving up. She was ungroomed, wore dirty clothing, and obviously had not bathed in quite some time.

The exorcist dressed in special garb, armed himself with religious objects, oil and water, and a special Bible or book. He kept praying, but once he started praying and reciting a particular prayer, the woman became physically restless. He kept insisting, over and over again, that the entity reveal its name. Once it finally did, the exorcist demanded repeatedly that the entity leave, along with intoning certain prayers that contained the entity's name, while additionally asking for her soul to return to her body.

To make a long story short, she began thrashing about with incredible strength, while verbally arguing with the entity within. In the meantime, the exorcist maintained his prayers and demanding that the entity leave, while we, the assistants, physically supported her to prevent self-harm.

This entire process took a couple of hours. Although difficult to explain in words, we knew when the entity finally left: it was almost as if an additional person had departed from the room.

The second one was a man. That case felt surreal in a sense, because the entity had more control over his body and personality. In fact, I was concerned for our physical safety because of his size. That one took many hours on the part of the exorcist and felt like the entity would never leave—it was tedious. The entity was harsh, threatening, insulting, and abusive. When it finally left, the man's face actually changed to a softer tone and his body seemed weak and frail.

The last time was a frail old woman, weighing about ninety pounds. The entity within her was provocative, and it knew things about me that nobody else knew. It was both embarrassing and demoralizing. It exposed my weaknesses and mocked them. Different voices came out of her mouth, and she was stronger than a mule. I was not expecting it—although I should have—when that little old lady lunged at me and threw a punch that left me with a busted lip. When this one was finally over, I had bruises all over my body and swore that I would never do this again.

Weeks later, I respectfully thanked the minister for all that he had taught me, but also told him that exorcisms were not my interest.

What did I really want to say to him? "Are you nuts? You have got to be out of your mind to be doing this, you crazy man! You want my help? Do you think I'm crazy too? Don't call me, I'll call you: BUH-BYE."

Yep, that's what I *really* wanted to say!

CONCLUSION

This is, and always has been, the sentimental stage of book writing because another journey, joined by all of you, is about to end. Hopefully, you have enjoyed reading this book as much as I have enjoyed writing it, but most importantly, my greatest desire is to have provided enough knowledge to improve your lives. If this has happened, then my goal has been fulfilled.

Please remember that our world appears to be equally balanced between good and evil. There are people, events, circumstances, energies, and even locations that fall into one of those two categories. Unfortunately, it is most often difficult to make a quick determination without first having all of the facts. Frequently, by the time we do know what we need to, if we have interacted with negative forces the damage may have been carried out. When this happens, the results will either be losing control and becoming susceptible to further harm or realizing that a mistake has been made. The best option is to embrace that mistake as a learning experience, repair the damage, and move on.

Even if we are well-protected and spiritually healthy, none of us are immune to interacting with the negative forces because they are equally present in the world. We will continue to encounter them and we will continue to make mistakes, but if our auras are healthy and maintained, the damage and recovery periods are minimal.

The most important aspect of this book is to remember that each and every one of us must trust our gut feelings. If you sense any "red flags," walk away rather than justifying the feelings, lowering your standards, and ignoring your God-given instincts. Know and love your self-worth. Two decades ago, I learned one of the most valuable life lessons from a Catholic nun, Sister Mary K: she taught me the meaning of knowing my own value.

When my husband passed away, his family alienated me, but this was by no means a hardship because I severely disliked those people! However, after having been dismissed by them for more than two years, one of his family members was stricken with metastasized cancer. She didn't contact me directly for help but instead appealed to my best friend Tom, who happened to be Catholic, in order for him to persuade me to give her free nursing care.

Tom immediately called and began reciting all these Bible passages out of context to make me feel like a sinner as well as a coldhearted, selfish person. He succeeded in making me feel very guilty.

Despondent, I discussed the situation with Sister Mary K, assuming that she would agree with Tom. But her reaction was quite the opposite. This even-tempered, tiny little lady I had always known was no more! Instead, she was infuriated by both the family member's boldness as well as Tom's disposition (as well as taking Bible verses out of context). Her response will never be forgotten . . . Sister Mary K said that God is within each and every one of us. When we allow people to take advantage of us, we are also allowing people to take advantage of God and that is the *true* sin. She ended her counseling with the words: "Stay away from that woman!"

Now, her message has been passed on to you: Respect yourself. Know your true worth. And protect your precious body and soul.

Allow me to express my gratitude to you for joining me on this journey: thank you!

You can find me on my website or on my Facebook page:

MissAida.com

Facebook.com/MissAidaPsychic

BIBLIOGRAPHY

Aida, Miss. *Cursing and Crossing: Hoodoo Spells to Torment, Jinx, and Take Revenge on Your Enemies.* Forestville, California: Lucky Mojo Curio Company, 2017.

Aida, Miss. *Destroying Relationships: Hoodoo Spells to Break Up, Separate, Hot Foot, and Drive off Your Foes and Rivals.* Forestville, California: Lucky Mojo Curio Company, 2018.

Andrews, Ted. *How To: See and Read the Aura.* St. Paul, Minnesota: Llewellyn Publications, 2003.

Bible Gateway. *BibleGateway.com.*

Catholic News Agency. "How can you tell if someone is demon-possessed?" *CatholicNewsAgency.com.*

CBS News. "How To Identify A Cult: Six Expert Tips." CBSNews.com.

Cunningham, Scott. *Cunningham's Encyclopedia of Magical Herbs.* Woodbury, Minnesota: Llewellyn Publications, 2009.

Dennis, Rabbi Geoffrey W. *Encyclopedia of Jewish Myth, Magic, and Mysticism.* Woodbury, Minnesota: Llewellyn Publications, 2016.

Hall, Judy. *The Crystal Bible: A Definitive Guide to Crystals.* Cincinnati, Ohio: Walking Stick Press, 2004.

Health Day. News for Healthier Living. "Illness: The Mind-Body Connection." *Consumer.HealthDay.com.*

Health Guidance. "Characteristics of a Sociopath." *HealthGuidance.org.*

The Holy Bible, King James Version, Rev. Edition, Thomas Nelson, Inc. 1976.

Illes, Judika. *Encyclopedia of Mystics, Saints & Sages: A Guide to Asking for Protection, Wealth, Happiness, and Everything Else!* New York: HarperOne Publications, 2011.

Illes, Judika. *Encyclopedia of Spirits: The Ultimate Guide to the Magic of Fairies, Genies, Demons, Ghosts, Gods & Goddesses.* New York: HarperOne Publications, 2009.

Inspirational Boost. "Nelson Mandela Famous Success Quotes." *Inspirationboost.com.*

Laremy, Robert. *Brazilian Palo Primer: Kimbanda Recipes to Make You Win at Love, Money, Business, and Life!* Old Bethpage, New York: Original Publications, 2002.

Mayo Clinic. "Narcissistic Personality Disorder." *MayoClinic.org.*

Mayo Clinic. "Stress Symptoms: Effects on Your Body and Behavior." *MayoClinic.org.*

MedCircle. "Narcissist, Psychopath, or Sociopath: How to Spot the Difference." *www.youtube.com.*

Melody. *Love Is in the Earth: A Kaleidoscope of Crystals— Update.* Wheat Ride, Colorado: Earth-Love Publishing House, 1995.

Moon, Hibiscus. "Crystals for Mercury in Retrograde." *Hibiscusmooncrystalacademy.com.*

Mortimer, Nigel. *UFOs, Portals & Gateways.* North Yorkshire, England. Wisdom Books Publications, 2013.

The National Center for Victims of Crime. *VictimsOfCrime.org.*

The National Domestic Violence Hotline. *TheHotline.org.*

National Suicide Prevention Hotline. *SuicidePrevention Lifeline.org.*

Psychic Library. "Beyond Books, Haunting Types." *PsychicLibrary.com.*

PsyWeb, Depression & Mental Health Resource. "Color Therapy for Depression." *PsyWeb.com.*

Simpson, Liz. *The Book of Chakra Healing.* New York: Sterling Publishing Company, Inc. 1999.

Tormson, David. "10 Insane Non-Religious Cults." *ListVoice.com.*

Wauters, Ambika. *The Book of Chakras.* Hauppauge, New York: Barron's Educational Series, Inc. 2002.

Wed MD. "Coping with Chronic Illnesses and Depression."
    WebMD.org.

Wikipedia. "September 11 Attacks." *En.Wikipedia.org.*

Wikipedia. "Spirit Possession." *Wikipedia.org.*

yronwode, catherine. *Hoodoo Herb and Root Magic: A
    Materia Magica of African-American Conjure.* Forestville,
    California: Lucky Mojo Curio Company, 2002.

Zaffis, John, and Rosemary Ellen Guiley. *Haunted by the
    Things You Love.* New Milford, Connecticut: Visionary
    Living, Inc., 2014.

ABOUT THE AUTHOR

Author and teacher, Miss Aida, was born into a Cuban family who practiced Santeria, Palo, and Brujeria. The practice of magic has always been a part of her life. Miss Aida is a natural-born medium and a Hoodoo practitioner, in addition to having received many initiations in Santeria and Palo. She is a registered nurse and a proud United States Air Force veteran. Miss Aida holds a master of science degree in health services administration. A renowned authority on Hoodoo, she is available for workshops, seminars, media presentations, as well as private psychic readings. Find her at *www.MissAida.com.*

TO OUR READERS

Weiser Books, an imprint of Red Wheel/Weiser, publishes books across the entire spectrum of occult, esoteric, speculative, and New Age subjects. Our mission is to publish quality books that will make a difference in people's lives without advocating any one particular path or field of study. We value the integrity, originality, and depth of knowledge of our authors.

Our readers are our most important resource, and we appreciate your input, suggestions, and ideas about what you would like to see published.

Visit our website at *www.redwheelweiser.com* to learn about our upcoming books and free downloads, and be sure to go to *www.redwheelweiser.com/newsletter* to sign up for newsletters and exclusive offers.

You can also contact us at *info@rwwbooks.com* or at

Red Wheel/Weiser, LLC
65 Parker Street, Suite 7
Newburyport, MA 01950